A HISTORY OF BIBLICAL STUDIES IN CANADA

SOCIETY OF BIBLICAL LITERATURE

BIBLICAL SCHOLARSHIP IN NORTH AMERICA

Kent Harold Richards, Editor

Number 7

A HISTORY OF BIBLICAL STUDIES IN CANADA
A Sense of Proportion

John S. Moir

John S. Moir

A HISTORY OF BIBLICAL STUDIES IN CANADA
A Sense of Proportion

SCHOLARS PRESS
Chico, California

SOCIETY OF BIBLICAL LITERATURE
CENTENNIAL PUBLICATIONS

The Society of Biblical Literature gratefully acknowledges a grant from the National Endowment for the Humanities to underwrite certain editorial and research expenses of the Centennial Publications Series. Published results and interpretations do not necessarily represent the view of the Endowment.

BS
586
.C2
M64
1982

Library of Congress Cataloging in Publication Data

Moir, John S.
    A history of biblical studies in Canada.

    (Biblical scholarship in North America, ISSN 0277-0474 ; no. 7) (Centennial publications / Society of Biblical Literature)
    Includes bibliographical references and index.
    1. Bible—Study—Canada—History. 2. Canadian Society of Biblical Studies—History. I. Title. II. Series. III. Series: Centennial publications (Society of Biblical Literature)
BS586.C2M64 1982   220'.07'071   82-5979
ISBN 0-89130-581-5   AACR2

Printed in the United States of America

To the memory of
James Frederick McCurdy, 1847–1935,
the father of biblical studies in Canada

Table of Contents

FOREWORD

Writing the history of a learned society might be seen as a routine job. Such histories are not a popular genre, and there are, I think, a few good models. So when it came time to prepare for the celebration of the fiftieth anniversary of the Canadian Society of Biblical Studies it was not clear how—or even whether—to write a history.

Fortunately John Moir, professor of history at Scarborough College in the University of Toronto, whose area of expertise is Canadian religious history, was interested in undertaking the task—as the history of the discipline. What has resulted is a model of clear historical analysis, written from the perspective of a Canadian historian rather than that of a biblical scholar. The perspective is thereby widened so that the resulting picture is set firmly in the social, cultural, and ecclesiastical history of nineteenth- and twentieth-century Canada.

The story has proven to have more intrinsic interest than any of us suspected. Many of the anecdotes are here described for the first time, dredged out of often overlooked archival materials and oral traditions. The developments in biblical studies share in the general developments of higher education in Canada, but there are also unique features that pertain to the particular form of church-state relationship that has evolved in Canada. As in so many aspects of Canadian culture, biblical studies in Canada did not fall neatly into the British or the Continental or the American mold in the early days. And as it has taken shape in the second half of the twentieth century it still remains *sui generis* One extremely important aspect of this unique character is the combination of French and English language biblical organizations which themselves reflect differing traditions and church roots. Professor Moir's insistence upon the importance, especially in the modern period, of these two traditions of biblical scholarship is a valuable contribution to the understanding of Canadian culture.

The links between Canadian biblical scholars, especially English-speaking ones, and the United States are strong. A large contingent of Canadians is always present at the annual meetings of the Society of Biblical Literature, and many Canadians have pursued their careers in the United States. A number of Canadian scholars have been presidents of the SBL, and it is fitting that the SBL publication program include this part of the history of American biblical scholarship in its centennial volumes.

Professor Moir has told the story as it looks to him as a historian. He has concentrated on the overall topic of the development of biblical studies as a discipline, and he has not dealt with certain questions that are of interest only to biblical scholars. The result is a sense of vibrant growth, of response to the shifting population centers, of fresh balances between religious traditions and languages of scholarship, of overall changes in emphasis, and of a new postwar accommodation to secularized education.

This is an account that covers a huge geographic area, a large time span, two cultures, and two subdisciplines. The overall shape and coherence of the story is a result of Professor Moir's encyclopedic knowledge of the period. The Canadian Society of Biblical Studies has every reason to congratulate itself on having commissioned him to write this history of biblical studies in Canada, just as it has reason to be grateful to the Society of Biblical Literature for publishing the volume in its centennial series. The result is a happy one, and the CSBS and the SBL have both been well served.

PETER RICHARDSON
University College
University of Toronto

PREFACE

When the Canadian Society of Biblical Studies asked me in 1975 to write the story of biblical studies in Canada, I was both flattered and apprehensive. I was flattered that my colleagues and friends in that field had such confidence in me, but I was apprehensive because as a mere historian I have so little knowledge of biblical studies. I was already convinced, however, that the story deserved to be told, that Canadian scholars had made significant contributions to the field of biblical studies over the last century and particularly since the founding of the Canadian Society of Biblical Studies fifty years ago. Although ignorant of the details of these contributions, I was aware as a historian that Canadian biblical scholars had earned international esteem. This has not been an easy book to write for several reasons, but the more I learned of the history of biblical studies in Canada the more I was convinced the book was a worthwhile, even necessary, undertaking. Now, six years later, the job is finished, despite the inevitable distractions of teaching but thanks to the generous help of many people who literally made its completion possible.

I must mention first those members of the Canadian Society of Biblical Studies who urged me to write—Peter Richardson, Robert Culley, Norman Wagner, and Peter Craigie—and also those associated with the Society of Biblical Literature who worked to see the manuscript transformed into print—Kent Richards and Douglas A. Knight, and Maurya Horgan and Paul Kobelski who copyedited incorrigible Canadian spelling and punctuation into conformity with the series style! Among my Canadian colleagues I must record my indebtedness to numerous biblical scholars—to Fred Winnett and Stewart McCullough, to R. B. Y. Scott, Ron Williams, Doug Tushingham, and John Wevers—all of whom gave generously of their time and knowledge toward my education. Special thanks are due to Bob Culley, David Stanley, and Adrien Brunet, who acted as readers and mentors of my manuscript on behalf of the Canadian Society of Biblical Studies, to Charles Anderson for sharing his knowledge of religious studies on the Canadian academic scene, and to all those members of the CSBS who provided me with biographical and bibliographical data.

Among the widespread company of Canadian archivists and librarians I am especially indebted to my friends Henri Pilon of Trinity College Archives and Mrs. Terry Thompson of the General Synod Archives of the Anglican Church in Canada, to Glenn Lucas and his staff at the Archives of the United Church of Canada, to my colleague David Rudkin and his staff at the University of Toronto Archives and Mrs. Susan Rice of the Archives of the Montreal/Ottawa Conference of the United Church of Canada, to Mrs. Lorna J. Hassell of Wycliffe College Library and Archives, to Robert Brandeis, Librarian and Archivist of Victoria College, to W. R. Mackinnon, Archivist of New Brunswick and to Olive M. Cameron of the Library of the University of New Brunswick, to Mrs. Kathy Gibson of Knox College Library, and to Mrs. Anne MacDermaid, Archivist of Queen's University. Several individuals must be mentioned here for the help they have provided—John Reid of Mount Allison University, Fred Stokes, Bursar of Victoria College, the Rev. Richard Ruggle for information on Anglican biblical scholars and Hans Rollmann of Memorial University for sharing his wide knowledge of German biblical scholarship, Robin Harris, historian of the University of Toronto, for access to special research information, and George Johnston, Keith Markell, Eric Jay and Stanley B. Frost of McGill University, and Stanley Walters of Knox College for offering the benefits of their wide experience in the field of history and biblical studies.

I want to make special mention of the support I received from Peter Richardson, Principal of University College and Secretary of the Canadian Society of Biblical Studies, whose advice was invaluable throughout the writing process; of a Canada Council Leave Fellowship which made possible the research in 1978–79; of the Office of Research Administration of the University of Toronto, whose financial support carried this project up to the stage of publication; of Paul Gooch, Chairman of the Division of Humanities, Scarborough College, who made research time possible; of my friend and editor Diane Mew, whose firm control over style and content imparted to the manuscript any literary competence it may possess; of Lois Pickup, who deciphered the work of the world's most hopeless typist; and of Angelica Demaria, who acted as my research assistant for one summer. Last and certainly not least I thank my wife, Jacqueline, who keeps a household of numerous children and almost as many dogs functioning smoothly and relatively quietly while I retreat to my study and she reads these proofs.

Having apportioned so much well-deserved credit, I regret that I must still personally accept the inescapable responsibility for all the sins of omission and commission that remain in the text.

JOHN S. MOIR
Scarborough College
University of Toronto

ABBREVIATIONS

KCA	Knox College Archives, Toronto
PChA	Presbyterian Church in Canada, Archives, Toronto
TCA	Trinity College Archives, Toronto
UChA	United Church of Canada, Archives, Toronto
UChA/MOC	United Church of Canada, Montreal-Ottawa Conference Archives, McGill University
UTA	University of Toronto Archives
WCA	Wycliffe College Archives, Toronto

I

A SANE AND TACTFUL COURSE

A sane and tactful course of Bible teaching . . . would do much to give college young men and women the right direction, and a sense of relative spiritual values in the most valuable single portion of their education.

                                                                    J. F. McCurdy, 1922

From Biblical Languages to Biblical Studies

In Canada the history of biblical studies dates from the 1880s, when the impact of German and British scholarship began to be felt in Canadian universities and seminaries and, consequently, in Canadian churches as well. For some three generations before that time the study of biblical languages had been offered in the curricula of theological institutions and to interested undergraduates who might be planning a career in business, law, teaching, or some other profession. Such studies were viewed as a useful and even desirable part of a liberal education in preparation for Christian living. This attitude, perhaps characteristically Canadian, was carried forward through the past century, and biblical studies, as opposed to the learning of biblical languages, came to hold a central place in the academic offerings of virtually every English-speaking Canadian university.

In contrast to the experience and tradition of biblical studies in Protestant and English-speaking Canada, French-speaking universities and seminaries and English-speaking Roman Catholic colleges have entered into the mainstream of biblical scholarship only within living memory. Although a seminary was established at Quebec city in 1668, there is no evidence that the study of biblical languages apart from Latin was pursued there or at other Roman Catholic seminaries at least until the mid-nineteenth century, and then only as a matter of personal interest rather than as part of the core curriculum. The Roman Catholic traditions of biblical literalism and emphasis on "sacrament" as opposed to "word" undoubtedly were the essential causes of this lack until the 1940s, but it must be remembered that in large measure French Canada was separated from its cultural roots in France, first by the British Conquest in 1763 and later by the triumph of irreligion during the French Revolution. Moreover, throughout the nineteenth and the first half of the twentieth century there was little or no intellectual contact between French- and English-speaking academic communities in Canada.

In colonial Nova Scotia, as later in New Brunswick and Upper Canada (Ontario), the development of biblical studies was deeply influenced by the local outcome of controversy over the "University Question," a political issue in the early history of higher education. In each instance, the "University Question" pitted supporters of church-related colleges against growing numbers of secularists who demanded nondenominational education and an end to any public aid for "religious" institutions. In the case of Upper Canada the "University Question" was embittered and protracted by the existence of a large land endowment. As a further complication the original creation of King's colleges—at Windsor, Nova Scotia, in 1788, at Fredericton, New Brunswick, in 1800, and at present-day Toronto in 1827—assumed that higher education should be a monopoly of the then-established Church of England. That assumption was soon boldly and successfully challenged in each colony by other denominations and rather less successfully by the secularizers.

A nondenominational provincial university, Dalhousie, was established for Nova Scotia in 1818, but teaching did not start until 1838. The fact that only Presbyterians were hired convinced many Nova Scotians that Dalhousie was not nondenominational. When its first president died in 1843, Dalhousie closed for a generation. The two small King's colleges and Acadia, a Nova Scotian Baptist foundation in 1828, were the only institutions in the Maritimes offering biblical languages, until the Wesleyan Methodists copied the Baptist example in 1858 by converting a preparatory school into Mount Allison University at Sackville, New Brunswick, strategically located on the border with Nova Scotia. In Nova Scotia the financial problems of King's and Acadia led to a demand for one provincial nondenominational college and for no public aid to sectarian institutions. In neighboring New Brunswick opposition to virtual Anglican control of King's at Fredericton prompted an investigation and eventually the college's "nationalization" and secularization in 1860.

Higher education in Upper Canada mirrored the trends in Nova Scotia but followed a decade later. Archdeacon (later Bishop) John Strachan's charter for King's at Toronto required the faculty to be Anglican but imposed no religious tests on students except those in divinity. Nevertheless, opposition to even this much Anglican influence led to the establishment of three denominational rivals—Queen's, a Church of Scotland college at Kingston, Regiopolis, a Roman Catholic foundation (which remained a preparatory school only) in the same city, and Victoria College, the Wesleyan Methodist institution at Cobourg. Almost as soon as Queen's opened in 1842 its principal approached Victoria with a proposal to seek a share of that provincial endowment being monopolized by King's. In the next five years four bills were introduced into the legislature on this matter—one proposed to secularize King's, the others to divide the endowment among denominational colleges. Strachan fought bitterly to keep King's and its endowment under his church's control, but opposing him and the leaders of the other religiously based colleges who wanted a share was a rising tide of secular reformism that sought to place all public funding beyond denominational reach. Strachan's efforts were doomed when the Reform party returned to power in 1848 with an overwhelming mandate for reforms in every area of provincial life. A year later the new government's program was unveiled, and it included the expected bill to transform King's into a secular and provincial "University of Toronto."

While these politico-educational battles were raging, King's had at last opened in 1843 and soon appointed Jacob Maier Hirschfelder to teach Hebrew. Born in Baden-Baden in 1819, Hirschfelder claimed to have studied at Heidelberg and in the Oriental school at Esslingen. He emigrated to Canada around 1837 and began teaching Hebrew, "Chaldee" (Aramaic), Syriac and Arabic in Montreal. In 1842 he was hired to teach Hebrew and German at a preparatory school in Toronto. Two years later he was appointed lecturer in Oriental languages at King's, and for the next three years he taught only Church of England divinity students. Then suddenly the size of Hirschfelder's classes increased substantially, and a major factor in the development of biblical studies in Canada entered the scene. The disruption of the colonial Church of Scotland in 1844 had been followed immediately by the creation of a Free Church theological college, Knox, at Toronto. In 1848 Knox arranged to have its students admitted to the Hebrew classes at King's—to the undoubted pleasure of Hirschfelder, who depended on fees of individual students for his income.

Unlike the Church of Scotland, whose educational philosophy melded "literary" and theological studies in a single institution, as at Queen's, the new Free Church was convinced that the two fields should be separated, that the state should have total responsibility for instruction in arts and sciences, and that the church should confine its teaching to theology. Thus, the secularization of King's in 1849 was welcomed by Free Church Presbyterians who were, not surprisingly, the Reform party's staunchest supporters. By the terms of the University of Toronto Act of 1849 no religious tests might be prescribed, no theology taught, and no clergyman serve as chancellor or president. The act offered nothing from the endowment to the denominational institutions, assuming that, faced with mounting financial problems, they would move to Toronto and act as residences or perhaps theological colleges. This dream of a single secular provincial university soon evaporated. "Despoiled" of King's, Bishop Strachan at the age of seventy-one established Trinity College in Toronto in 1852 as an unquestionably Anglican institution. Meanwhile, Victoria and Queen's managed to survive at Cobourg and Kingston.

The granting of Trinity's charter by the crown negated the government's centralizing plan, and at the same time fewer students attended the university each year as public confidence in a "godless" institution waned.

The secularist aims of the reformers did not agree with the views of Canadian society that generally saw no conflict between the ideals of separation of church and state and the sharing of the provincial endowment among all foundations of higher learning. In response to criticism of the university the reformers compromised in 1853 with an act that transferred the teaching functions to a new and nondenominational University College, an admission that centralism and secularism had failed to win support from a community more British than American in its religious attitudes.

Not only did the older institutions, Victoria and Queen's, survive to mock the failure of the secularists, but in addition to Trinity a number of other new denominational colleges sprang up in the next decades. In 1857 the Baptists opened the Canadian Literary Institute (Woodstock College), and in the same year the Methodist Episcopal church established Albert College at Belleville. At about the same time the strong evangelical movement that had disrupted the Church of Scotland prompted controversies between high and low church Anglicans. These led to the opening of Huron College at London in 1864, Wycliffe College in Toronto in 1877, and of Diocesan Theological College, Montreal, in 1873, to train "low church" clergy. Evangelical Protestant interest in biblical languages was also part of the violent anti-Romanist response to "Papal Aggression" and the subsequent religious conflicts in British North America. Freedom to read and interpret scripture became a central issue in these confrontations and a weapon in the active crusade to convert French Canadian Roman Catholics to Protestantism.[1] Evidence of this missionary impulse was the Presbyterian College, established in Montreal in 1865 by the Free Church in part to train French-speaking ministers.

Throughout this half century when Hebrew and related languages were taught under an older and conservative dispensation, largely uninfluenced by the ferment of higher criticism that was building in Germany, Britain, and the United States, Jacob Hirschfelder stands out because of his long association with the University of Toronto and also because, unlike most Canadian teachers of biblical languages in that period, he published books. His first volume, *The Scriptures Defended* (Toronto, 1863), was an assertion of the Mosaic authorship of the Pentateuch; his second, *The Spirit and Characteristics of Hebrew Poetry* (n.p., n.d.), was adopted as a textbook at the University of Toronto, at Albert College, and elsewhere.[2] His last and most important work was a two-volume *Biblical Expositor and People's Commentary* (Toronto, 1882, 1885), which elaborated on his Old Testament

---

[1] E. C. Woodley, *The Bible in Canada* (Toronto: J. M. Dent & Sons, 1953) p. 38. For background to the religious and educational conflicts of this period see J. S. Moir, *Church and State in Canada West* (Toronto: University of Toronto Press, 1959) pp. 13–26, 82–115.

[2] F. V. Winnett and W. S. McCullough, *A Brief History of the Department of Near Eastern Studies (formerly Oriental Languages) in the University of Toronto to 1976–1977* (Toronto: Department of Near Eastern Studies, 1978?) p. 6.

historical interpretations and explanations. Hirschfelder also designed the early program of Oriental literature offered at the University of Toronto, in which Hebrew (using Gesenius) was available for credit in all four years, Aramaic (based on Winer's *Grammar*) in the third and fourth years, and Syriac, Arabic, and Samaritan in the final year only. The loss by fire of the university's records make it impossible to know the size or composition of his classes, but in addition to candidates for the ministry (presumably with a majority from Knox) there may have been some students who enrolled from interest and, as the curriculum became more permissive after 1863, some who took Hebrew as an option.

By the middle of the nineteenth century Hebrew and usually some cognate languages were offered at most Protestant colleges (both arts and theology) and in the provincial institutions as well, yet the subsequent development of critical biblical studies extended into few of these institutions. A survey in 1860 of courses and textbooks used in theological education by the seven largest denominations (Church of England, Church of Rome, Church of Scotland, Canada Presbyterian [Free] Church, Wesleyan Methodists, Baptists, and Congregationalists) reveals the low priority assigned to biblical languages. Only the Church of Scotland reported that Hebrew was a requirement—Wolfe's *Hebrew Grammar* was the only textbook used—but the Baptists required New Testament and Septuagint Greek, and both the Wesleyan Methodists and the Free Presbyterians used T. H. Horne's *Introduction* to biblical criticism. More pertinent to the situation in the universities, a supplementary list of courses and texts at the University of Toronto, Victoria, Queen's, and Trinity made no reference to biblical languages in their undergraduate programs, even though such courses might be available as options.[3]

As early as 1853 a degree of specialization in teaching responsibilities had begun to appear at University College, in contrast to the continuing practice in other institutions, especially church-related ones, of requiring instructors to display simultaneous versatility in several disciplines. Although this trend toward specialization was not widely evident until the 1880s, by then it owed much to the Canadian admiration for the contemporary German emphases on specialization of knowledge and commitment to research. However, it was indebted more to the availability of funds, to the gradual separation of arts instruction from theology, and, in the case of the church-related colleges, to the sympathy and support of college officers and governing bodies. Ultimately, of course, much depended on the ability of the teachers of Oriental literature and history to pursue "a sane and tactful course" while introducing disturbingly new ideas to a deeply religious and conservative community. The founding of chairs, such as Joseph Flavelle's

---

[3] H. Y. Hind, *Eighty Years' Progress in British North America* (Toronto: L. Stebbins, 1863) pp. 440–43, 463–67.

endowment of a chair of Hebrew at Victoria in 1905 with a subscription of $25,000, marked the formal recognition of specialization.

In making this transition to specialization only Victoria and University colleges seem to have had all the requisites at that period, and even then the growth of biblical studies under the aegis of higher critics did not always pass unchallenged. Victoria was deliberately a literary institution; Methodist ministers were normally trained on the job although college-educated preachers had become less of a rarity by the 1860s. Even the Methodist theological training did not emphasize languages; candidates did not need Latin, Greek, or Hebrew. Preaching was their primary requirement, and one president complained that those who failed in the pulpit were then sent to Victoria![4]

Student interest in biblical languages at Victoria was suddenly and permanently aroused, however, by the appointment in 1866 of Nathaniel Burwash, a graduate of the college, who had done his theology at Garrett Biblical Institute in Illinois and had taught Hebrew in a private school. Perhaps because of his presence the college calendar for 1867–68 listed for the first time the texts used in biblical language classes—Arnold's *First Book* for Hebrew and Green's *Grammar* and *Chrestomathy* for Greek. After Burwash's arrival the breadth and depth of biblical courses at Victoria expanded markedly. When a theological faculty was established in 1870, the second-year course included Greek Testament and Hebrew, but the bulk of biblical studies was still being offered in the undergraduate arts faculty. Officially Burwash was still professor of natural science until 1871, when he became professor of Hebrew and biblical literature in arts, and dean and professor of theology. The biggest changes in biblical studies at Victoria, however, still lay ahead—the organization of a department of Oriental languages in 1881 and the appointment of George Coulson Workman as associate professor of Hebrew in 1882.

The creation of separate undergraduate departments of Orientals at Victoria in 1881 and in University College at Toronto five years later was only one feature of the new era dawning on biblical studies in the closing decades of the century.[5] More important results of that earlier phase of widespread teaching of biblical languages were two trends foreshadowing future Canadian developments in the field. First, Hirschfelder was working in a supposedly secular institution rather than a church college or seminary, yet this intermixing of biblical and profane subjects was accepted as natural and even normal by most contemporaries thanks to the uncritical and largely uncriticized fusion of religion with national life. Second, within the religiously affiliated colleges there seemed to exist a mildly liberal approach

   [4] *On the Old Ontario Strand: Victoria's Hundred Years* (Toronto: Victoria University, 1936) p. 130.
   [5] UTA, Loudon Papers, M25, J. F. McCurdy to James Loudon, undated.

to biblical studies based on the postulate that such studies promoted appreciation of the Bible as long as they were governed by common sense and obvious personal piety. Darwinism, "modernism," and higher criticism (Canadians preferred to call it historical criticism) had as yet produced minimal reactions in British North America, but the ideas unleashed by these movements could not be ignored indefinitely. In the last score of years in the Victorian era a new generation of scholars was emerging that absorbed much of contemporary European scientific, philosophical, and biblical research and reflected those influences clearly in the distinctive Canadian academic experience and in the intellectual life of the Christian community of the country.

The Impact of "Modernism"

Drawing on a literary image familiar to Americans, J. Loewenberg has written, "Charles Darwin fired a shot heard round the theological world."[6] By the time the echoes of that shot, *On the Origin of Species*, reached the forested colonies of British North America, however, the sound fell very faintly on a few academic ears. A. B. McKillop has described the reception of Darwin in Canada as consisting essentially of two reviews by William Dawson and Daniel Wilson.[7] Dawson, the theological geologist of Nova Scotian, Presbyterian origins, rejected as wrong Darwin's special variation into a law of special diversity. Such "wild and fanciful applications" of inductive science violated the Mosaic account of creation. Wilson, the literary scientist, rejected Darwin's evolutionary theory not on religious but on methodological grounds, namely, the lack of supporting evidence from geology. The immediate impact of Darwinism in Canadian intellectual circles was minimal indeed, and among the securely orthodox population at large it must have been indiscoverable.

A greater colonial reaction might have been expected to *Essays and Reviews* (1860), since some of its articles involved direct attacks on verbal inspiration of the scriptures, but again there is little evidence of awareness of the volume, much less of any influence on contemporary Canadian opinion. More important, to the extent that reaction was measurable, was Bishop John William Colenso's *The Pentateuch . . . Critically Examined* (1863), which occasioned Hirschfelder's *The Scriptures Defended*. None of these publications had much effect on biblical studies in Canada. Nevertheless, within a generation the cumulative results of the new biblical studies in Britain and more especially in Germany would become apparent in the Canadian academic scene. The twin evidences of this change are the

---

[6] J. Loewenberg, "Darwinism Comes to America, 1859–1900," *Mississippi Valley Historical Review* 28 (1941–42) 350.

[7] A. B. McKillop, *A Disciplined Intelligence: Critical Inquiry and Canadian Thought in the Victorian Era* (Montreal: McGill-Queen's University Press, 1979) pp. 99–100.

expanded role of biblical studies in college curricula beginning about 1880 and the emergence of a group of Canadian scholars and teachers, trained in the most rigorous methodology and moderately liberal interpretation of biblical studies.

Canadians and, particularly, Canadian Presbyterians were well acquainted with the controversy that had flared in Scotland between 1876 and 1881 around Julius Wellhausen's former student, W. Robertson Smith. Smith's article on the Bible in the *Encyclopaedia Britannica* had caused his rejection in Scotland and his acceptance at Cambridge, leading T. K. Cheyne to comment, "The Professor won this battle for others, not for himself."[8] In fact the Robertson Smith case had reputedly caused many Canadian theological students to read his books and, according to W. G. Jordan a half century later, "made them realize the importance of the views which up to that time had not received much attention here."[9] Canadians also followed with deep interest the trial of Charles Briggs and his deposition from the Presbyterian ministry in the United States a decade after the Robertson Smith affair. The Briggs case stirred uneasy feelings among some Canadians, not because it was geographically closer to home but because it gave further evidence of the inroads being made by higher criticism into academic and church circles.

Despite these concerns, Canadians extracted from German influences and philosophic trends of the age what suited or pleased them best—in biblical studies the carefully delimited conservatism of Franz Delitzsch at Leipzig seems to have set the norm for Canadian scholarship. During the last quarter of the nineteenth century at least nineteen Canadians did postgraduate biblical studies abroad. Some of them studied in more than one country, Germany and the United States being the most popular places. Fifteen attended German universities (nine of them at Leipzig); Edinburgh attracted four; and one went to Oxford because he could not afford to study in Germany. American institutions including Yale, Harvard, Princeton, and Chicago were the choice of ten of the Canadians. Eight of the nineteen received Ph.D.'s abroad—three from Leipzig and one each from Heidelberg, Breslau, Edinburgh, Yale, and Princeton. Another dozen Canadians seem to have completed all their postgraduate studies at home. Ten others who taught biblical studies in Canada were not Canadians—three were originally Cambridge students and two each came from Oxford and Edinburgh, while only one was American.

The interesting feature of these probably incomplete statistics is the predominant influence of Germany and particularly of Leipzig and Franz Delitzsch. By the close of this second phase in the growth of biblical studies

[8] Quoted in W. G. Jordan, "The Higher Criticism in Canada. II. The Canadian Situation," *Queen's Quarterly* 36 (1929) 31.

[9] Ibid., 32. See also R. A. Raesen, "'Higher Criticism' in the Free Church Fathers," *Records of the Scottish Church History Society* 20 (2, 1979) 119–42.

in Canada the pattern of postgraduate studies abroad and especially in Germany created a kaleidoscope of both Canadian and external influences. The "Leipzig connection" and German preponderance began to decline around the turn of the century for several reasons, none of which can be readily documented. After the death of Franz Delitzsch in 1890, Leipzig was less of a lodestone for North Americans, particularly as other institutions developed special fields of biblical studies. But the lure of German universities generally also may have declined in the face of increasingly strained German-British relations after the turn of the century. In place of the romantic ideal of pan-Germanism a new trans-Atlantic linking of the English-speaking peoples was developing, based on close physical, political, economic, intellectual, and spiritual liaisons that had grown since the American Civil War. The emergence of postgraduate biblical studies in American universities and particularly at Chicago toward the end of the Victorian era provided an alternative for Canadian students seeking further education.

Returning to Canada to teach the next generation, these foreign-trained scholars were able "to harmonize their Christianity with the discoveries of science. Thus, the Canadian universities were able to maintain the essential compatibility of religious truths and scientific theories."[10] Higher criticism could now be introduced and generally accepted as a respectable adjunct to orthodox faith. Perhaps the introduction was made with mental reservations or even equivocations in some quarters, but, nonetheless, historical criticism developed gradually with little fanfare and surprisingly little opposition or public outcry before the turn of the century. In part the Canadian denominations received the newest learning because its purveyors were generally scholars of proven piety, not to mention good sense. The transition, however, undoubtedly raised some suspicions, and in at least three instances involving theological colleges, advocates of "modernism" and "fundamentalism" came into conflict. Two of these cases, that of John Campbell at the Presbyterian College and that of George C. Workman of Victoria, received wide publicity.

Workman was born near Cobourg in 1848 and graduated from Victoria with his B.A. in 1875 and his M.A. in 1878. Four years later he was hired to teach metaphysics and theology at Victoria, where he displayed a certain fussy sensitivity and "a desire to impress which much impaired his usefulness."[11] In 1884 Workman went on leave "for a couple of years" to prepare himself for teaching Old Testament and Orientals to Victoria's

[10] P. Roome, "The Darwin Debate in Canada, 1850–1880," in *Science, Technology, and Culture in Historical Perspective*, ed. L. A. Knafla et al. (Calgary: University of Calgary, 1976) p. 199.

[11] C. B. Sissons, *A History of Victoria University* (Toronto: University of Toronto Press, 1952) p. 193.

theological and arts students.[12] Instead he spent most of the next five years and almost his last dollar studying at Leipzig with Franz Delitzsch. From there he instructed Victoria's staff and students through the pages of *Acta Victoriana* with adulatory accounts of all things German—from student singing in beer gardens to the piety and dedication of God's annointed kaiser. His highest praise was reserved for the scholars of Leipzig University, in particular Franz Delitzsch the Assyriologist, his son Friedrich the Hebraist, Ernst Curtius the Hellenist, Ernst Windisch, professor of Sanskrit, Georg Ebers the Egyptologist, and H. L. Fleischer, "the greatest Arabic scholar in Europe."[13] In a eulogistic obituary of the elder Delitzsch, Workman described his own experiences in the master's classes, in his "exegetical society," and in his private study. Delitzsch was "a man of simple habits, of generous impulses and of refined tastes . . . a man of deep piety, of broad culture and of profound scholarship . . . in Biblical criticism, he was a Liberal Conservative."[14] He had also provided a laudatory introduction for Workman's first book, *The Text of Jeremiah* (Edinburgh, 1889), which he called "a work of valuable and lasting service" by "my Canadian friend."[15]

In 1890, Workman's first year back at Victoria, he was invited to give the annual lecture to the college's Theological Union, a society of theological graduates who allowed undergraduates to attend their session. His lecture received wide press coverage since it was delivered as part of Convocation Week. His theme was "Messianic Prophecy," which, he explained, was not specific Old Testament predictions of the coming of Jesus but only expressions of traditional Jewish hopes for the appearance of a national savior-king. The audience was most favorably impressed with his display of scholarship, as were the college students and many in the Methodist church, but this opinion was not shared universally. Toronto newspapers reported the lecture under sensational headlines and soon voices were heard in official circles condemning heretical teaching at Victoria.[16] E. H. Dewart, editor of the official Methodist paper, *The Christian Guardian*, led the attack with a 256-page book, *Jesus the Messiah in Prophecy and Fulfilment: A Review and Refutation of the Negative Theory of Messianic Prophecy* (1891).

Workman was not without his defenders, but so many accusing letters reached Victoria's board of regents that the issue could not be avoided

[12] Victoria College, Bursar's Office, Minutes of the Board of Regents and Annual Meetings, p. 279, 6 May 1884.
[13] *Acta Victoriana* 8 (1885) 6; see also ibid., February, March, April 1885, for other installments of Workman's reports.
[14] Ibid. 13, no. 7 (April 1890) 7–8.
[15] G. C. Workman, *The Text of Jeremiah*, pp. xxii, xxi.
[16] Tom Sinclair-Faulkner, "Theory Divided from Practice: The Introduction of the Higher Criticism into Canadian Protestant Seminaries," *Canadian Society of Church History, Papers 1979*, pp. 43ff.; Nathaniel Burwash, *The History of Victoria College* (Toronto: Victoria College Press, 1927) pp. 40–49; Sissons, *History of Victoria University*, pp. 192–93.

indefinitely. After a seven-page typewritten response from Workman (in which he declared that he had no sympathy "with assumptions of radical and extreme critics" and that his purpose was to make "the ancient prophets . . . live and speak again . . to men of modern times"), the board at its meeting in January 1892 heard his oral defense and resolved that since Workman had recently repeated his "objectionable positions" regarding messianic prophecy, he should not teach theology at Victoria. Burwash tried a mollifying amendment accepting Workman's protestations of orthodoxy and "the expectation that the exercise of his best judgment will prevent undue prominence of controversial theories in his teaching."[17] Two more amendments later the board reaffirmed by a ten to eight vote its decision to move Workman to arts, whereupon Workman submitted his resignation from Victoria.

However moderate Workman believed he was, his expressed opinions in biblical matters were still too advanced for many, perhaps most, Canadian Methodists. His case had been closed by the college authorities, but the reverberations continued both inside and outside his church. At Victoria a farewell party given for him by the students was attended by faculty and friends. There Principal Burwash called for "liberty of investigation and discussion" in theology, and the students' address to Workman strongly denied charges that the popular professor had had "a baneful effect upon the spiritual life of your students."[18] His very moderate reply to this address (in which Workman reiterated that he had been misunderstood) was frequently interrupted by cheers. After prolonged applause subsided, Burwash was invited to speak. Sensing the danger of a student protest against the board, he defused the situation by praising Workman as "a Christian gentleman and a scholar" and, expressing regret at the board's action, called for "more liberty of investigation and more tolerance among Christians for the views of others." Perhaps even as he spoke Burwash recalled the words of S. R. Driver's review of Workman's *Text of Jeremiah* in 1889, that Workman's judgments were "crude, superficial and inconsistent, and he is greatly deficient in the faculty of discrimination."[19] Perhaps too he remembered Workman's opposition to university federation in 1886, when Workman had publicized his fear that "state-paid, . . . sceptical and unprincipled Professors" might undermine instruction that required "the light of revealed truth"![20]

The case of John Campbell of Presbyterian College differed at least to the extent that Campbell was only a dilettante in biblical studies. The

[17] Victoria College, Bursar's Office, Minutes of the Board of Regents and Annual Meetings, pp. 75–76, 6 January 1892.
[18] *Acta Victoriana* 14, no. 4 (January 1892) 16–17.
[19] *Expositor* 3d series 9 (1889) 336.
[20] *Acta Victoriana* 9, no. 8 (May 1886) 5–6.

professor of church history and apologetics had published articles in such assorted places as the *Princeton Review* and the *Canadian Naturalist,* but his main claim to fame—aside from a difficult personality—was the two-volume work, *The Hittites, Their Inscriptions and Their History.* His passion for the Hittites later led him into uncharted waters when he tried to prove a linguistic affinity between the Hittites and such widely dispersed groups as the Japanese, central African tribes, and the Indians of the British Columbia interior. In 1893 Campbell gave a public lecture at Queen's entitled "The Perfect Book and the Perfect Father," wherein he declared his belief in a literal devil but denied the inerrancy of scripture. In due course he was charged by the Presbytery of Montreal with heresy for his view of scripture and his insistence that God does not judge. Until his case was heard he was prevented from teaching, and both his supposedly "liberal" colleagues, Principal Daniel MacVicar and John Scrimger, professor of Old Testament, supported the charges because "duty to God, to the truth and to the Church comes first."[21] The Presbytery found Campbell guilty, but this judgment was reversed on appeal to Synod when Campbell agreed to a typically Canadian compromise statement that some parts of the Old Testament were "not the whole truth" and that God judges "in the great majority of cases."[22] The fact that Synod, unlike Presbytery, was dominated by former students of Campbell may have influenced the final verdict when only three votes were recorded against him.[23]

Historically Campbell's case is similar to Workman's in several ways. In both instances it was not so much the content of the "heretical" statements as the dogmatic presentation and defense that brought down fire on both scholars. Any such statement offered as an abstract theory or as an academic question deserving investigation might have passed unchallenged. Again, in both cases, but particularly in Workman's, there was confusion of academic freedom of inquiry and speech with the right and responsibility of a denomination to maintain and defend its own doctrinal standards. Workman's case attracted much greater attention and had more far-reaching effects largely because he was vocal and popular in a way that the eccentric Campbell never was.

The third instance occurred at Diocesan Theological College in Montreal, where Frederick Julius Steen, a graduate of the University of Toronto and of Trinity College, had become the second member of faculty in 1896 at the age of twenty-eight. Two years later he was made a special preacher at the nearby cathedral and soon attracted large audiences of young people. "His sermons were simple in character but in them he frequently touched upon the results of recent investigations and modern

---

[21] *Presbyterian Review,* 10 August 1893, p. 73.
[22] Ibid. 15 March 1894, p. 655.
[23] *Presbyterian College Journal* 24 (1904) 56.

discoveries which had thrown new light on certain biblical statements and he explained in simple language, in what way and how far, these new discoveries had confirmed, illuminated or modified conceptions or beliefs which had been formerly held."[24] Suddenly in 1901 Steen was forced by the board of the college to resign his professorship, the only explanation offered by the principal being that his teachings on revelation and inspiration were "open to question."[25] When Bishop W. B. Bond, chairman of the board, also prevented him from preaching, it became obvious that Steen's high church sympathy for higher criticism was not acceptable to his low church diocesan and older members of the cathedral congregation. The Steen case had a divisive effect on Montreal Anglicanism but affected parish relations more than those of the college. Steen died in 1903, and the affair was largely forgotten by later generations.

University Federation at Toronto

Although political reformers and secularists had failed to create a single, centralized university for Upper Canada during the 1850s, the idea was revived by the fact of confederation in 1867, since education became a purely provincial matter under the British North America Act. The "University Question" was discussed intermittently and inconclusively in Ontario until 1881 when William Mulock was elected chancellor of the University of Toronto. The first change in the situation came that year as St. Michael's College affiliated with the university; four years later Wycliffe, Knox, and the Toronto Baptist College (forerunner of McMaster University) also affiliated. For biblical studies the most immediate result of these developments was the university's acceptance of biblical Greek, biblical literature, and four other religious subjects as options for third- and fourth-year students. Affiliation, however, was only a preliminary step to a solution of the "University Question." In 1883 Mulock publicly proposed expansion of the University of Toronto using public funds. This evoked an immediate response from Queen's and Trinity that such a plan was unfair to the other arts institutions. The denominational colleges were still suffering from the depression that had started in the early 1870s and once the idea of possible increased funding was mentioned the whole University Question was bound to be reopened.

Victoria College reacted somewhat differently. It was prepared to seek a compromise based on genuine federation among equals, which would thus create a united "Christian University."[26] After epic discussions with its board, alumni, and the Methodist church, Victoria agreed in 1886 to

---

[24] F. D. Adams, *A History of Christ Church Cathedral* (Montreal: Burton's, 1941) p. 100.

[25] Oswald Howard, *Montreal Diocesan Theological College: A History from 1873* (Montreal: McGill University Press, 1963) p. 49; Adams, *History of Christ Church Cathedral*, pp. 101–2.

[26] N. Burwash in *The Mail*, 3 December 1883.

federate with the University of Toronto. Henceforth Victoria would confer only theological degrees, would teach primarily languages and religion-related subjects (leaving other disciplines and professional training to the university) in return for financial support. In the words of Victoria's most recent historian, "The provincial Act embodied the principle that religion has a place in education that must be recognized and defined in any truly national system."[27] The physical transfer of Victoria from Cobourg to Toronto was completed in 1892, and the federation was joined by Trinity in 1903 and by St. Michael's in 1910. For each college the terms of federation differed slightly, but each retained the authority to teach undergraduate biblical studies in its arts program. Queen's rejected federation as early as 1885 and has remained in Kingston. McMaster, successor in 1887 to the Toronto Baptist College, also rejected federation, and after living next door to the university for two generations moved to Hamilton in 1930 to have room for expansion.[28]

The Toronto federation meant a concentration of academic resources, human and material, on a scale unprecedented in Canada and probably in North America. In addition, the university had access to the libraries and occasionally the faculties of Knox and Wycliffe. Federation was admittedly accomplished in stages, because the denominational colleges joined at different dates, and St. Michael's did not effectively enter into biblical studies until after World War II. Nevertheless this concentration of resources and the unique amalgam of religious and secular institutions combined to place the University of Toronto historically in the forefront of the development of biblical studies in Canada at least a generation ahead of any of its sister universities. The interchange of students between colleges for the purposes of instruction certainly strengthened biblical studies at Toronto, and the subsequent development of graduate biblical studies based on the Orientals department of University College (the graduate section called "Semitics") was vital for national and international recognition of Canadian biblical scholarship.

In this development of the discipline the appointment of James Frederick McCurdy to teach Orientals in University College has justly been taken as a starting point for the history of critical biblical studies in Canada. McCurdy's teaching career at Toronto began at the dawn of Canadian biblical studies and closed literally on the eve of World War I, providing a unifying thread to the story. Born in 1847 in a Presbyterian manse at Chatham, New Brunswick, he received his B.A. from the University of New Brunswick in 1866 and a year later entered Princeton Theological College.

---

[27] Sissons, *History of Victoria University*, p. 182.

[28] Hilda Neatby, *Queen's University, Volume I, 1841–1917* (Montreal: McGill-Queen's University Press, 1978) pp. 160ff.; C. M. Johnston, *McMaster University, Volume I/The Toronto Years* (Toronto: University of Toronto Press, 1976) p. 41 and passim.

He graduated from there in 1871 but remained another eleven years, nine of them as assistant to W. H. Green and, significantly for his later career, supervisor of the college's linguistic program, teaching Hebrew and Sanskrit. McCurdy received an honorary Ph.D. from Princeton in 1878 and three years later published *Aryo-Semitic Speech: A Study in Linguistic Archaeology*. He was, however, both independent of mind and liberal in his opinions—he was the only person at Princeton to join the recently organized Society of Biblical Literature and Exegesis.[29] When he was criticized by conservative colleagues for a paper read at Johns Hopkins in 1882 on evolution and the history of language, "it seemed an opportune time to remove from an institution with whose point of view he must have been increasingly out of sympathy" and to go abroad and study.[30] The next two or three years he spent at Göttingen and at Leipzig, where he studied under the two Delitzsches, E. Schrader, and P. A. de Lagarde, taking a particular interest in Assyriology.

McCurdy returned to Canada in 1885, settling at Toronto where he received an appointment in 1886 as tutor in Oriental languages at University College. No document concerning his appointment seems to have survived, but it is reasonable to assume that he was chosen to understudy and soon replace Hirschfelder, who was then in his late sixties. Three years later when Hirschfelder did retire after a year's leave of absence, McCurdy was immediately promoted to professor and head of the Department of Oriental Languages, at a salary of two thousand dollars. The *Knox College Monthly* commented on this appointment: "Under his direction we may expect to see the important department over which he presides make satisfactory advancement. In Professor McCurdy, Knox College has a tried friend . . ."—he was after all a Presbyterian and a son of the manse, and in 1884 over 40 percent of the university's students were Presbyterian![31]

McCurdy's promotion was certainly central to the development of biblical studies in Canada. McCurdy represented the best in contemporary scholarship and was a dedicated, thorough, and inspiring teacher who trained a brilliant collection of young Canadians in rigorous methodology and liberal principles while imparting a reverence for scripture. He capped his solid academic reputation with a three-volume magnum opus, *History, Prophecy and the Monuments*, that appeared in 1894, 1896, and 1901. The publication of volume one was marked by the conferring of an honorary LL.D. by his alma mater, the University of New Brunswick, and on

[29] E. W. Saunders, "A Century of Service to American Biblical Scholarship," *Bulletin of the Council on the Study of Religion* 11 (1980) 70.

[30] *University of Toronto Monthly*, October 1935, 1–13. Reference to McCurdy's honorary degree is supplied in a letter of C. A. McClelland, Princeton University Archives, to W. S. McCullough, 22 June 1977, with enclosure, in the possession of W. S. McCullough.

[31] *Knox College Monthly* 9 (1888) 99; H. H. Langton et al., *The University of Toronto and Its Colleges, 1827–1906* (Toronto: University Library, 1906) p. 117.

completion of the final tome W. G. Jordan wrote in a review for *Queen's Quarterly*: "The significant thing about this volume is that the author, one of Dr. Green's most distinguished pupils, accepts cordially and unreservedly 'the documentary theory' of the Pentateuch against which the great Princeton scholar fought so valiantly to the very last."[32]

Part of McCurdy's influence must have stemmed from the peculiar arrangements in the university federation at Toronto. Because University College was "godless" only in the sense that it had no denominational affiliation, McCurdy was free to develop Orientals as a valid and respectable discipline in its own right within the university's curriculum. Henceforth the offering of biblical languages would be much more than a "service course" for future ministers. At the same time University College was never "religionless"—cynicism or even skepticism about the authenticity and value of the higher religions was unthinkable to its Christian professors, of whom McCurdy was a natural leader. From the time of his arrival in Toronto he belonged to St. Andrew's Church and was a close friend, admirer, and biographer of its famous minister, Daniel James Macdonnell, who earlier had been accused of heresy because of his expressed doubts over eternal punishment.[33]

Settled at University College, McCurdy lectured seventeen hours per week, teaching almost fifty first-year students, twenty-three second-year, and ten more in the third and fourth years combined, out of a total student population of some five hundred.[34] His workload increased after 1888 when the department began to offer an honors course. Arabic became a prescribed course for third year and Assyrian for fourth, and Hebrew was made an alternative to French or German in all four years of undergraduate studies. The total program was designed by McCurdy at the request of Principal William Caven of Knox College and Principal J. P. Sheraton of Wycliffe.[35] A Ph.D. program in Orientals had been proposed even before McCurdy joined the faculty, but such an ambitious undertaking was postponed until 1897 by the board of governors.

If McCurdy was overworked, so were several other professors in University College and their complaints led to an investigation. The committee reported in the spring of 1891 and, regarding Orientals, pointed out that McCurdy was unable to provide the additional nine lecture hours that the committee deemed requisite, because he was working single-handedly. Help

---

[32] Quoted in Jordan, "Higher Criticism in Canada," p. 37.

[33] J. S. Moir, *Enduring Witness: A History of the Presbyterian Church in Canada* (Toronto: Presbyterian Publications, 1974) pp. 172–74.

[34] A full account of the state of the Department of Orientals in 1891 is given in McCurdy's written submission to a university commission. See *University of Toronto and University College. Revenue Requirements. Report of a Committee appointed by the Senate of the University of Toronto, and also by the Board of Trustees, April 13th, 1891*, particularly pp. 58–59, 89–92.

[35] UTA, Falconer Papers, Box 78, J. F. McCurdy to Sir R. A. Falconer, 4 September 1922.

was forthcoming almost immediately. David William McGee, a former student of Hirschfelder and McCurdy, was hired as a lecturer. McGee, a native of Owen Sound, received a Ph.D. from Breslau in March 1895, but four months later he drowned in a boating accident at the age of twenty-three. Perhaps a year before McGee's death McCurdy had reported to the new university president, James Loudon, on the past achievements and future needs of his department. The teaching of biblical studies at Toronto, he asserted, "now stands on a level with Harvard, Johns Hopkins, the University of Pennsylvania, and the University of Chicago." The employment in the department of a professor and a lecturer was admittedly in part to serve "the large and increasing number of students" proceeding from arts into the Christian ministry, but Orientals were also of popular interest "as a branch of general culture" because of Semitic contributions to the origins of science and art, as well as religion. Semitic studies were now being "more generally cultivated in accordance with the enlarged views and broader sympathies of modern scholarship and thought." "Nor can we forget that the Bible itself, whose study as *literature*, should form part of the curriculum of every college, is from beginning to end an Oriental book." Would it not therefore be desirable, he concluded, to merge Oriental languages, philology, and ethnology into a single professorship?[36]

While McCurdy was busy teaching and planning in University College, biblical studies at Victoria and Trinity were making forward strides. Workman's replacement at Victoria, again chosen from within the faculty, was John Fletcher McLaughlin, another Ontario-born graduate of the college and gold medalist in metaphysics who had been teaching science there since 1888. McLaughlin was in some ways an unexpected choice; he was as much a liberal as Workman and, if more circumspect in the way he presented higher criticism, still attracted opposition from conservative clergy on occasion. He must already have had a reputation as an agitator, since he had been temporarily expelled from Victoria on the eve of his graduation for criticizing one allegedly incompetent professor.[37] McLaughlin, released from teaching to spend three years upgrading his knowledge of biblical languages, settled in Oxford under the direction of S. R. Driver. His sojourn abroad was cut short in 1893, however, by an urgent request that he return to teaching after Workman's sudden departure.

The choice of McLaughlin for biblical studies at Victoria was important for the college and for the development of the discipline in Canada. During the next forty years he taught and wrote, placed his graduates on the faculty of every Canadian Methodist college, and earned international recognition

---

[36] UTA, Loudon Papers, M25, J. F. McCurdy to James Loudon undated (but, from internal evidence, before McGee's death).

[37] UChA, J. F. McLaughlin Papers, microfilm, J. F. McLaughlin to Emily Gimby, 1 April 1888; Nathaniel Burwash, *History of Victoria College*, p. 408.

for his scholarship. Victoria had also acquired a professor of New Testament as part of the expansion of biblical studies at the time of Workman's appointment. Francis Huston Wallace, a son of the manse but now a Methodist, had graduated from the University of Toronto in 1873, had done further studies at Knox, Drew Theological Seminary, and Leipzig, and had published a book, *Witness to Truth*, two years before his appointment. His reputation as a teacher and administrator earned Wallace the post of dean of theology at Victoria in 1900.

At Trinity College, by contrast, biblical studies held no special place in either the arts or theological departments. In 1883 a new and reputedly rigorous course in theology was introduced that allowed for specialization to meet the need for more scholarly research in the face of attacks on Christianity.[38] At the same time Hebrew grammar and the translation of "easy Biblical passages" became a second-year option, and the final examination in Oriental languages was extended in arts to include Aramaic and Syriac. These changes probably owed much to the influence of the provost, Charles William Edmund Body, who arrived at Trinity in 1881. A Cambridge graduate, Body had also attended the Tyrwhitt School of Hebrew. In 1894 he published *The Permanent Value of Genesis*, but that same year he left Trinity for the General Theological Seminary in New York City. His successor, Edward Ashurst Welch, was another Cambridge graduate via King's College, London, who served as provost until 1909. He made no mark on biblical studies and his real contribution to Trinity was leading the college toward federation with the University of Toronto. Such a move had been long and strongly opposed by many of Trinity's staunchest supporters, although the college magazine had loudly defended secular University College when McCurdy arrived. "This epithet [godless]," it commented, "cannot be justly applied to a College, the students of which are largely drawn from four Divinity Halls and support a Young Men's Christian Association."[39] The statement in itself was evidence of the growing consensus on the necessary place of religion in higher education.

A Growing Discipline

Where the three major universities at Toronto—Toronto, Victoria and Trinity—could boast the presence of McCurdy, McLaughlin, and Body in their undergraduate programs, the affiliated theological colleges—Knox and Wycliffe—were confined to studying biblical themes within a theological context, and in the case of Wycliffe that meant within a strongly conservative and evangelical milieu generally unsympathetic to higher criticism. Knox continued to supply a steady stream of students at both undergraduate

---

[38] *Rouge et Noir* 4, no. 3 (March 1882) 11.
[39] Ibid. 6, no. 2 (April 1885) 12.

and graduate level to McCurdy's classes, while at the same time it took a
long step toward specialization with the appointment of Robert Yuille
Thomson to a newly established chair of Old Testament. Born in Scotland,
Thomson had entered the University of Toronto in 1871, and after graduating from arts and from theology at Knox he spent a term at Heidelberg and
a year at New College, Edinburgh.[40] After four years in the pastorate he
began lecturing at Knox in 1887, spent a summer at Göttingen, and was
promoted to the new chair in 1890. Thomson's teaching career was relatively brief, however, as his health was so undermined by severe study
habits that he died just four years later. In that short time Thomson had
introduced Knox College to the stream of contemporary biblical studies.
Knox's alumni, solidly grounded in Orientals by McCurdy's department and
further awakened to the current work of higher critics by Thomson and his
successors, were in the front ranks of Canadian liberal biblical scholarship
over the next three decades and were conspicuous among the students who
made the academic pilgrimage to Germany and Scotland before World
War I.

Thomson was succeeded, although only for two years, by George
Livingston Robinson, an American who had studied at Princeton, Berlin,
and Leipzig and later shared in the discovery of Petra. Unlike Thomson or
Robinson, however, Knox's third appointment in Old Testament was destined to be of major importance for the development of biblical studies in
Canada. John Edgar McFadyen, a twenty-eight-year-old Scot who had
studied at Glasgow, Oxford, and Marburg and had married a German
woman, was hired by Knox in 1898. He had taught classics for four years
and Old Testament literature at the Free Church college in Scotland for one
year while completing his theological studies. He graduated in 1898 with the
highest standing among all Scottish theological students that year. For
Canadian biblical scholars the addition of McFadyen to their ranks was an
event of great promise, a promise more than fulfilled during the first decade
of the new century.

At neighboring Wycliffe College all biblical work and much else was
still taught by Principal Sheraton who, in addition to academic and administrative duties, edited *The Evangelical Churchman*. At his death in 1906 he
was lauded as "the best Hebrew scholar" after Provost Body among Anglicans of Ontario.[41] Like so many of his contemporaries in seminary teaching
Sheraton had little time, incentive, or opportunity to write for publication.
His first monograph was the conservatively oriented *Inspiration and
Authority of the Holy Scriptures* (1893), and in 1904 he published *The
Higher Criticism and Our Lord's Teaching Concerning Himself*. Sheraton

[40] KCA, Knox College Senate Minutes, 1894–97, pp. 9–12, 27.
[41] Quoted in *The Enduring Word: A Centennial History of Wycliffe College*, ed. Arnold
Edinburgh (Toronto: University of Toronto Press, 1978) p. 15.

did start Wycliffe toward curricular specialization by hiring Henry John Cody in 1884 as professor of the literature and history of the Old Testament. A native son of Ontario and graduate of the University of Toronto, Cody had not as yet given any hint of the heights of political and academic power he would reach in later years, including the provincial cabinet and twelve years as president of the University of Toronto. His involvements in public life were always numerous, and combining a curacy with teaching at Wycliffe until he resigned the latter position in 1899 further constrained scholarly research and publication.

In McMaster University (which opened in Toronto in 1887 as the main Baptist arts and theology center) liberal biblical scholars were in evidence from the beginning of the institution. The tone was set by William Newton Clarke, who was professor of New Testament interpretation at the older Toronto Baptist College from 1883 until that institution was transformed into McMaster. Clarke, who has been described as "the Schleiermacher of American theology,"[42] was the author of nine volumes including *An Outline of Christian Theology* (1894), which went through at least twenty editions, and of *Sixty Years with the Bible* (1912), a largely autobiographical work. At McMaster, New Testament was taught after 1891 by the liberal, modernist, social gospel proponent Jones Hughes Farmer, a native of Perth, Ontario, and gold medalist in classics at the University of Toronto in 1878. Farmer, who spent two years at the conservative Southern Baptist Theological Seminary before returning to Canada, had as a colleague Calvin Goodspeed, a native of New Brunswick who had studied in the relatively liberal atmospheres of Andover Newton and Leipzig. Goodspeed published *The Messiah's Second Advent* in 1901.

Beyond the Toronto scene biblical studies had made scant progress by the end of the century. Where the larger institutions were able eventually to appoint one or more biblical experts to faculty, many of the smaller colleges relied on the part-time services of local clergy to complete their course offerings. Of the five institutions in Montreal—McGill University, Congregational, Wesleyan Theological, Diocesan Theological, and Presbyterian colleges—only one had a teacher who was influential in promoting higher criticism before Steen's five-year stint at Diocesan. John Scrimger, colleague at Presbyterian College of the difficult John Campbell, had been born in Galt, Upper Canada, in 1849. A brilliant product of the famous Dr. Tassie's Collegiate Institute there, Scrimger entered the University of Toronto on scholarship, graduated with first class honors and silver medals in both metaphysics and modern languages, and a year later entered Knox College, where he graduated first in every subject with almost every prize for which he was eligible.[43] While

---

[42] C. H. Pinnock, "The Modernist Impulse at McMaster University, 1887–1927," in *Baptists in Canada*, ed. J. K. Zeman (Burlington, Ont.: G. R. Welch, 1980) p. 197.

[43] *Presbyterian College Journal* 1, no. 4 (April 1881) 30.

serving a Montreal pastorate Scrimger doubled as lecturer in Presbyterian College from 1874 until his appointment to the recently endowed chair of Greek
and Hebrew exegesis and sacred literature eight years later.[44] At his induction
as professor, Scrimger was charged to observe the boundaries and philosophy
of biblical studies as seen by contemporary Canadian Presbyterians.

> You go to your Chair untramelled by conditions or traditions. It is your business to find
> out what the Spirit has said in the Word, irrespective of the Babel of conflicting
> creeds. . . . If your unbiased investigations into the grammatical and historical signifi-
> cance of the several parts of the Word are found to harmonize with the creeds, all
> good and well; but it is not to be your aim to make them speak rightly or arrange the
> language of the creeds. . . . But while you will no doubt be on your guard against the
> many subtle sources of misleading, to which our surroundings necessarily subject us, as
> to the proper interpretation to be put on the Word of God, I am equally confident that
> you will avoid the opposite, and more objectionable, extreme of striving to find star-
> tling novelties in the way of interpretation.[45]

Interestingly, Scrimger's students commented on his all-Canadian education: "The truth must be told, . . . he never studied in Germany . . . and
[has] not taken an 'extra session' in the Old Country. . . . Think of it, ye
votaries of fashion who worship with your faces towards the East."[46]

Scrimger showed himself to be both discreet and progressive. As early as
March 1884, an unsigned article by him in the *Presbyterian College Journal*
denied that science and the Bible were in conflict. In a signed item for the
same periodical in 1897 entitled "Recent Discussion in Old Testament
Criticism," Scrimger offered "a report of progress" (which was also an apolo-
gia), "with a view to placing those who are not able to follow these
discussions closely . . . in a position to understand something of the present
situation and of the general trend of thought." Describing the arguments
about hexateuchal authorship he praised C. A. Briggs, S. R. Driver, and
A. Plummer for their International Critical Commentary—"the best vindication of the Wellhausen Theory of the Pentateuch.' His own disagreement
with the conservatives was evident in his criticism of Baxter, and Green of
Princeton, who may have assisted McCurdy's return to Canada. Scrimger,
however, pointed to the discoveries of biblical archaeologists as instrumental
in convincing some textual critics of the historicity of the Old Testament,
even if Wellhausen still held that early Jewish history was "largely a
fabrication." As the article continued—it was twelve pages long—Scrimger's
differences with the evangelicals became more obvious.

> With many evangelicals it has become a sort of fixed principle that the whole subject is
> simply a product of rationalizing scepticism, which cannot be too severely reprobated
> and denounced, that it is a device of unbelieving men to undermine the authority of
> the Bible. . . . Many still living can remember how geology was denounced as a foe of

[44] Ibid. 6, no. 7 (April/May 1886) 214–16.
[45] Ibid. 3, no. 1 (October 1882) 4.
[46] Ibid. 1, no. 4 (April 1881) 30.

religion, and how Darwin's 'Origin of Species' was regarded as the chief infidel book
of the day. It is surely the veriest stupidity for the friends of Christianity to allow
themselves to be stampeded by every unfamiliar sound, and to suppose the ark of God
to be in danger every time the cart is unexpectedly shaken. . . . Biblical criticism is a
genuine science, and must be treated as such.[47]

In the Maritimes the picture of biblical studies was disheartening.
Oriental languages were still being taught at Acadia and Mount Allison
(Dalhousie and the University of New Brunswick apparently offered nothing
in the field), but none of the instructors earned reputations as scholars and it
is uncertain how far, if at all, their courses reflected current trends in biblical studies. One exception, in a sense, was Robert Alexander Falconer at the
Presbyterian church's Pine Hill Divinity Hall in Halifax. Falconer was yet
another "son of the manse," born on Prince Edward Island and educated in
the West Indies, London, Edinburgh, Leipzig, Berlin, and Marburg, who
had been appointed to New Testament at Pine Hill in 1892 and had
received an honorary LL.D. from the University of New Brunswick at the
age of thirty-three. Falconer's importance lay not in his scholarship but in
his popularity as a writer and public speaker, as an administrator, and as an
officer in many social organizations. It was this public image that later
earned him the presidency of the University of Toronto, where he gave full
support to McCurdy and to McCurdy's campaign to make his department
paramount in biblical studies in Canada.

Two institutions in Winnipeg—the Presbyterians' Manitoba College and
Wesley College—offered Oriental languages in their theological faculties.
At Manitoba College, John Mark King, an Edinburgh graduate who had
studied in Halle, Berlin, and Marburg, was principal and professor of
theology from 1883 to his death in 1899 and was considered a representative of the German tradition in biblical scholarship. His teaching covered
theology, moral and mental science, and German, but also Greek and
Hebrew exegesis and Oriental languages and literature. These last subjects
King must have shared with Andrew Browning Baird, another of
McCurdy's students who had gone to Leipzig, earned an Edinburgh Ph.D.
in 1881, and joined the staff of Manitoba in 1887 to teach Old and New
Testament exegesis and Oriental languages and literature and later Hebrew
and church history. Baird's only publication was *Notes on Introduction to
the Old Testament* (1898), which opposed higher criticism. At Wesley
College, Andrew Stewart began teaching Old and New Testament exegesis
and Oriental languages and literature one year later than Baird. Both
apparently retired officially in 1919 (although Stewart was still giving
classes in Orientals as late as 1925), and neither contributed substantially to
the development of biblical studies.

In retrospect the development of biblical studies in Canada during the last

---

[47] Ibid. 17, no. 1 (November 1897) 1–13.

two decades of the nineteenth century manifested certain characteristics that were to mold its course through the next fifty years. The most obvious of these characteristics was the hegemony of the Department of Orientals at the University of Toronto. That increasing dominance stemmed partly from the dedication and ambition of J. F. McCurdy, partly from the peculiar situation in that university, where biblical studies were pursued intensively at the undergraduate level within an institution that was nominally secular. But the success of McCurdy in building his department and of biblical studies in University College grew first from the unique arrangement of theological colleges in physical proximity to and working partnership with the provincial university. The established practice of training future clergy in Orientals within Hirschfelder's classes was expanded by university federation, which allowed for the broadest interchange of students among the colleges. Federation also reinforced the acceptance of biblical studies as an academic subject in its own right rather than a mere service course from budding theologians. Undoubtedly the collecting of the various faculty members and bibliographical resources in biblical studies under the umbrella organization of federation was an additional encouragement to scholarship.

One characteristic of that period which did not endure was the heavy dependence of young Canadians on European and especially German universities for postgraduate work in the field of biblical studies. With the new century such scholars found new and reputable centers for continuing study closer to home and even in Canada. For them the focus of academic interest in the biblical field shifted westward across the Atlantic to settle primarily at Chicago and Toronto. Here the liberal tradition and practices of higher criticism found new and congenial homes. The Canadian churches at least until after the turn of the century accepted and even welcomed the "modernist" trend, providing always that its exponents were reverent and orthodox in their approach, pursuing what McCurdy described as "a sane and tactful course" in presenting proven facts, not imaginative theories, and always with tender regard for popularly accepted beliefs. If Steen, Campbell, and Workman had fallen into trouble in the theological colleges on account of their views of scripture, it was as much because of their dogmatic and flamboyant methods of presentation as it was because of the debatable content of their message.

Contributing to this relatively easy reception and assimilation of the new biblical learning by the Canadian public was what Robert Handy has described as the "churchly" religious outlook of the nation. In a country where 85 percent of the population belonged to just four denominations (Roman Catholic, Presbyterian, Methodist, and Anglican) a tradition of toleration and openness balanced any tendency toward conservative biblicism. To this fact must be added the successful popularization of higher criticism through literature and through the unquestioned piety of Canada's higher critics themselves who, along with their disciples, spread the message discreetly from hundreds, perhaps thousands, of pulpits. As the twentieth century opened the institutional groundwork was already prepared, the trained scholars on hand, and the public attitude receptive for the full flowering of biblical studies in Canada.

II

FRANK, SCIENTIFIC DISCUSSION

Now you know that I have never been afraid of the most frank scientific discussion of O. T. literature, but I am aware that if we are not to injure the Oriental Department we must go carefully just now.

Sir Robert Falconer, 1912

McCurdy's Young Men

Biblical studies in Canada during the last decades of the nineteenth century had been marked first by the hesitant emergence of criticism from the early stage of uncritical biblical language study and second by the work of J. F. McCurdy—the father of biblical studies in Canada—an inspiring teacher and, equally important, the architect of the Department of Orientals at University College in the University of Toronto Under McCurdy's tutelage Orientals had grown from Hirschfelder's small "service" department into an autonomous and recognized discipline of major importance, religious in its materials and interpretation but secular in its academic setting. In the first two decades of the new century Canadian biblical studies were characterized by the virtually unchallenged dominance of the field by McCurdy's department and his students. As Orientals rooted and grew at Toronto, biblical studies at other Canadian institutions were so far outstripped as to give the appearance of a virtual monopoly of the discipline at Toronto and its affiliated church-related colleges. Outside Toronto, biblical studies did not develop significantly until after World War I.

A second change in direction for biblical studies in Canada had already cast its shadow in the closing years of the Victorian era. Postgraduate studies in German universities, and particularly at Leipzig, were losing their fascination for Canadians primarily because the new generation of German scholars was more extreme in its biblical liberalism than its predecessors. Canadians had also developed such confidence in their national educational institutions that postgraduate work at a Canadian university was accepted as a learning experience equal or at least not markedly inferior to that available at older European institutions. Beyond this sense of self-awareness and self-assurance Canadians could and did travel with increasing frequency to study at the University of Chicago, whose prestige as a center of biblical studies had risen meteor-like and remained fixed high in the North

American academic firmament. After 1900 Canadian biblical studies were open to more external influences than ever before, and not the least of these influences were the work and personalities of such Chicago scholars as Shailer Mathews and Canadian-born Shirley Jackson Case.

McCurdy's influence and his academic ambitions for his small department were reflected not merely in the success of his graduates in their studies abroad but also in the development of graduate work in Orientals at the University of Toronto despite pressure to abandon this work because of a chronic shortage of funds. The details for a Ph.D. program had finally been adopted in 1897 after a twelve-year incubation, and the first degree was awarded in 1900. In the next five years three of the fourteen Ph.D.'s granted by the university were given in biblical studies, and Orientals was the first department in the humanities to have graduates of the program. The first such degree went to Ross George Murison in 1902 for his eleven-page study "The Mythical Serpents of Hebrew Literature." That same year Richard Davidson was awarded his doctorate for research entitled "The Semitic Permansive-Perfect," and in 1905 Irish-born Thomas Eakin received his Ph.D. for the study "The Text of Habakkuk, Chap. I, 1–II, 4."

Murison had been born about 1870 in Aberdeenshire, Scotland, and was orphaned in childhood. He came to Canada at the age of nineteen and worked his way through college as a railway navvy, completing the Toronto B.A. in 1893, the Knox certificate in theology in 1894, and his M.A. the following year. He had won a university entrance scholarship by learning Greek in only six days! At Knox College his scholarly interests and habits earned him the sobriquet "the Rabbi" from his fellow students. Murison spent 1895–96 studying in Germany and was awarded a B.D. by Knox at the end of that academic session. Apparently Murison was appointed to lecture in Orientals at University College in 1894 and took up these duties again on his return from Germany. In the next decade he produced what for that time must have been a prodigious number of published works, including his Ph.D. thesis through the University of Toronto Press, brief histories of Egypt and of Babylonia and Assyria for an Edinburgh publisher, an article on totemism in the Old Testament for *The Biblical World*, and one on his thesis topic for the *American Journal of Semitic Languages*. For a wider audience he wrote articles on Babylonian banking and law in the *Canadian Banker's Journal* and the *Canadian Law Review*. As early as 1896, when he succeeded the ill-fated McGee as lecturer, a Toronto newspaper hailed him as a "brilliant young scholar,"[1] and a year later he was advanced to the rank of assistant professor. Suddenly, in September 1905 Murison's promising career was cut short when he contracted typhoid fever and died in a matter of days.

The loss of Murison understandably touched McCurdy deeply. A scholarship in Orientals was established in memory of the thirty-five-year-old teacher

[1] *Mail*, 26 September 1896.

whose life had had so much of the Horatio Alger about it. Since Murison's death occurred just at the opening of the academic year, it was necessary to find an immediate replacement, and McCurdy's choice was Murison's classmate Richard Davidson. Born at Ayr in southwestern Ontario, Davidson received his B.A. from University College in 1899, finished his M.A. at Toronto a year later, and graduated from Knox College in 1901 with a traveling scholarship that took him to the University of Berlin for two years. While doing his doctoral studies under McCurdy, Davidson was a special lecturer at Trinity College. He taught at University College in 1904–5, then two years at Presbyterian College, Montreal, before he returned to replace Murison.

Since Davidson could not leave Presbyterian College until the end of term in 1906, Murison's work was taken up for that intervening year by Thomas Eakin, another Presbyterian who had received his Ph.D. in Orientals under McCurdy. An Ulsterman by birth, Eakin had come to Canada in 1891 and received his M.A. from Toronto and his ordination in 1897. Before his return to scholarly pursuits he had spent six years in the pastorate. Along with Eakin a second instructor was hired for the year, and again he was a Presbyterian. Calvin Alexander McRae was born in southern Ontario in 1874 and spent some years in business before he enrolled at the University of Toronto. By 1905 he had obtained his M.A. and also graduated from Knox College, and during those college years he managed to get two summers at the University of Chicago and two years in Germany, and to lecture in both Arts and Divinity at Trinity College. Davidson, like Murison, was a favorite and protégé of McCurdy, but his stay in the Department of Orientals at Toronto lasted only four years because he accepted the Old Testament chair in Knox College in 1910 as successor to J. E. McFadyen. To fill the gap left by Davidson, Eakin was promoted to associate professor and McRae returned as a special lecturer. McRae's connection with the department again lasted only one year because he left permanently in 1911 and returned to the Presbyterian pastorate.

One development of importance for McCurdy and his department and for biblical studies generally in Canada was the appointment of Robert Alexander Falconer (later Sir Robert) as president of the University of Toronto in 1907 immediately after a new University Act transformed the board of governors from a collection of political appointees to a collection of successful (but not necessarily apolitical) business leaders. Falconer epitomized that new breed of administrators in both state and church-related Canadian colleges whose primary concern was good public relations for their institutions. Where President James Loudon had been politically inept, Falconer moved adroitly through legislative, business, and academic labyrinths, promoting the interests of his institution, sometimes at the expense of both faculty and student concerns. For a quarter century he served successfully as the politic and political president of the university, ever protective of its good name and eager to enhance its reputation. He had published a major New Testament work, *The Truth of the Apostolic Gospel* (1904) and hoped to produce a volume of Greek letters in translation,[2] but his presidential duties and public involvements virtually ended his own scholarly career. As president, however, Falconer showed himself a sympathetic and dependable supporter of McCurdy's ambitions for biblical studies at Toronto.

Another development of great and lasting importance for biblical studies was the establishment of the Royal Ontario Museum. Chancellor Burwash had hoped to employ one of Victoria's graduates, C. T. Currelly, then a student of Sir Flinders Petrie, to collect antiquities for a college museum. When this proved financially too ambitious, J. F. McCurdy urged that the university, rather than the college, create such a museum. He enlisted the aid of Edmund Walker, a college friend of Currelly and a very successful banker who was also chairman of the board of governors.[3] The future of the project depended on the attitude of the opinionated Samuel H. Blake, who, to the surprise of his fellow governors, became its enthusiastic advocate. Soon after Currelly was empowered to collect for the museum, McCurdy asked him to get "two or three Assyrian tablets, as he had a good-sized class in cuneiform and none of them had ever seen a tablet."[4] With his usual touch of the flamboyant, Currelly brought him over four hundred tablets from an English collector to start the important Near Eastern collection of the Royal Ontario Museum. Over the years the museum became a treasure-house of such materials and a research center of international importance, thanks to the work of Currelly at various archaeological sites and among international dealers in antiquities.

In all these comings and goings of personnel in the Orientals department, the close connection between McCurdy and Canadian Presbyterianism stands out. Obviously the other two major Protestant denominations—the Anglicans and the Methodists—felt their interests in biblical studies were being met through their own colleges, particularly Trinity and Victoria in Toronto, so that McCurdy's seeming preference for Presbyterian scholars in his department could be viewed as an extension of the long-standing connection between Knox College and University College. On the other hand it is strange that no voice was raised in objection to the apparent policy of the Presbyterian president of the university and of his Presbyterian colleague, the chairman of Orientals, to staff that department exclusively with their coreligionists, however talented those young scholars might be.

[2] UTA, Falconer Papers, Box 33, H. T. Duckworth to Sir R. A. Falconer, 28 January 1915.
[3] C. T. Currelly, *I Brought the Ages Home* (Toronto: Ryerson, 1956) pp. 38, 129–30.
[4] Ibid., p. 264.

Biblical Studies in a "Godless" College

At Toronto a critical incident specifically involving the Department of Orientals and the teaching of biblical studies developed in the wake of the new University Act of 1906. After a third of a century in power, the provincial Liberal government had been defeated at the polls in 1905 and the new Conservative premier, J. P. Whitney, a friend of the university, immediately launched a seven-member royal commission to propose a new system for operating the university federation The main thrust of the subsequent legislation was intended to shield the university from direct political interference by creating a buffer in the form cf an appointed board of governors. The provincial statute was "an attempt to introduce organic unity into a body which has been built up by successive accretions, and which has suffered in the past from a resulting division of authority."[5]

The crisis involving biblical studies hinged on the interpretation and implementation of Section 127(2), which directed University College to give instruction in "Oriental Languages" among other listed subjects, "but not in theology," and of Section 129(10]—"The curriculum in Arts of the University shall include the subjects of Biblical Greek, Biblical Literature, Christian Ethics, Apologetics, the Evidences of Natural and Revealed Religion and Church History, but any provision for examination and instruction in the same shall be left to the voluntary action of the federated universities and colleges. . . ."[6] The ambiguity of this phraseology was directly responsible for the dispute, since it was not clear whether University College could teach the subjects intended in the "curriculum in Arts of the University." The new act had barely become law when the controversy was initiated by Samuel Hume Blake, younger brother of the renowned jurist-statesman, Edward Blake (the only Canadian politician born in a log cabin), who, ironically, had been chancellor of the university from 1873 to 1900. S. H. Blake, a prominent Toronto lawyer, governor of the university, cofounder of Wycliffe College, and a strident champion of a rigid and aggressive evangelicalism opened his campaign for value-free education with a letter published in the *Mail and Empire* on 13 December 1906.

> The university was established and is maintained for the purpose of teaching secular subjects only. The classics, Oriental and modern languages, mathematics, science, literature, history, etc. It is to teach these subjects and to teach them in such a way that the very varied religious convictions of its supporters shall suffer no hurt, that the University is maintained, and no professor has a right to teach anything else. He may be an Anglican, or he may be an infidel, a Methodist or a Roman Catholic, but he must keep his convictions to himself. . . .

[5] H. H. Langton, ed., *The University of Toronto and its Colleges, 1827–1906* (Toronto: The University Library, 1906) p. 263.
[6] Ibid., pp. 324–25.

Just two years later Blake had convinced himself that his worst fears regarding University College had in fact been realized. On 30 November 1908 he wrote to John Hoskin, chairman of the board of governors, complaining that religion was being taught in University College contrary to the terms of the recent act. Hoskin replied to Blake two weeks later in general terms, suggesting that Blake had been misinformed. The offending classes were in fact offered by the Semitic Language Department (another title for Orientals) and involved only biblical literature with "no dogmatic teaching and no work of interpretation being carried on." Hoskin denied that students were lured into these courses with "substantial scholarships" and that enrollment was declining because of students withdrawing from the classes. He closed in a highly humanistic vein with the assertion, "It would seem necessary that a properly equipped University should take some cognizance of literature which is ranked with the most important any nation has given to man."[7]

At first glance the point at issue might appear to be legalistic, but the deeper motivation came from the seventy-three-year-old Blake's violent reaction to liberal biblical studies: "The first objection I heard made was from a Student who ceased to attend because of the heterodox teaching he found in the class [on Religious Knowledge]." He itemized his eight charges in a two-thousand-word rebuttal to Hoskin. The classes *were* being offered by a new "Department of Religious Knowledge," and the calendar descriptions did employ such phrases as "Natural Theology," "evidences of the Christian Religion," and "evidences of . . . Christian Doctrine."

> When the text books to which the student is referred by the Professors . . . are those of Driver, Bennett, McFadyen, and Kent, written expressly to give dogmatic interpretation according to the teaching of radical criticism, then all doubt on the aim and purpose of this instruction disappears and those finding fault with the "Department of Religious Knowledge" have the added ground of complaint that not only is such instruction given but it is of the class strongly objected to by many supporters of the University.[8]

Further, the question of the "Virgin birth" had been discussed in classes of the department, and this had drawn "a stern reprimand" from university authorities. No fewer than four scholarships were offered "for Biblical Literature," and students with conservative leanings *had* quit the courses. The public who financed the university would not allow such teaching to pass unchallenged. Apart from the objectionable nature and illegality of such teaching, it was a waste of money "to duplicate work which may be done more efficiently and under proper supervision by affiliated Colleges whose function it is to perform the same." As for Hoskin's motherhood appeal on behalf of biblical studies, Blake noted:

---

[7] WCA, O'Meara Papers, S. H. Blake to John Hoskin, 22 December 1908.
[8] Ibid.

There is a very wide difference between taking "some cognizance of the literature" and the using this liberty as an opportunity to assai the authenticity of the Bible, to introduce and advocate the views of the higher critics, to instill a disbelief in the Messianic character of Old Testament prophecy, and to introduce the idea among Students that large portions of the Bible, accepted by many as God's Word, are mere myths or allegories and to be rejected as "old wives' fables."[9]

Seeking allies for his cause, Blake invited the reactions of Chancellor Burwash of Victoria College to his letter to Hoskin. Burwash agreed that the teaching about which Blake complained was "*ultra vires*" in University College." "I am sorry that it should be transferred to the department of Orientals, as, if this work is done at all, it should not come in by any back door." Burwash did not, however, seem as exercised about the matter as Blake thought he should be. In a twenty-five-hundred-word reply Blake informed Burwash, "The mistake you appear to me to make is, in assuming that because certain options in Theological subjects are included in the *curriculum* of the University . . . the University has liberty to *teach and examine* in such subjects!"[10] Blake continued—quoting a Latin aphorism to imply that Burwash was a traitor to his college's interests—but more than half of the letter was filled with fundamentalist statements regarding biblical interpretation, substantial quotes from John Wesley and the Bible to support this position, and criticism of "the so-called higher critics and scientists." "No, my dear Chancellor, I abhor the thought that our Toronto University should aid in the work of shaking men's confidence in the Bible as being the Word of the living God. . . ." Blake ended with two challenges—let Burwash rise in defense of the exclusive privileges of the federated colleges, and let the higher critics make "a positive statement" of their biblical beliefs for the benefit of "the laymen, whose money is demanded to support such instruction. . . ."

Apart from Blake's use of Burwash's words, no written evidence of the opinions of the federated colleges seems to have survived. (In his letter to Hoskin on 22 December, Blake quoted an anonymous authority from one of these institutions supporting his arguments.) Such an anti-intellectual attack from a powerful and visible source could not, however, be ignored with impunity. A special committee of the board of governors (chaired by the Reverend Donald Bruce Macdonald, a Knox graduate, principal of St. Andrew's College preparatory school and member of the royal commission that had produced the University Act of 1906) reviewed Blake's three letters and heard testimony from McCurdy, Eakin, Davidson and University College principal, Maurice Hutton. Also interviewed were conservatives William McLaren, principal of Knox College, Dr. Albert Carman, general superintendent of the Methodist church in Canada, and Dr. Elmore Harris, scion of the agricultural implement family (Massey-Harris, now Massey-Ferguson), pastor

---

[9] Ibid.

[10] Ibid.; S. H. Blake to Nathaniel Burwash, 11 February 1909.

of Walmer Road Baptist Church, founder of the Toronto (now Ontario) Bible College and an outspoken opponent of liberalism wherever discovered. Harris left a paper on the question in dispute in the hands of the committee—the others simply agreed with Blake that the nub of the issue was the interpretation of Section 129 of the University Act. Since the working documents of the board's committee are apparently lost, Harris's testimony must be summarized as the claim that the 1906 act "excludes all interpretation of the Bible through any of the professors or lecturers of University College, whether in the form of Higher Criticism, Lower Criticism, or any other criticism."[11]

Already controversy had reached the public through the columns of the Toronto *Star*, an inveterate critic of the university. On 6 March Blake's letter to Burwash was printed along with a statement from Harris that students were being indoctrinated with the "most radical type of Higher Criticism." Privately Blake wrote to Wycliffe College's principal, T. R. O'Meara, deploring what was happening in Canada's colleges: "I feel more and more convinced that the great battleground today is over God's Word. . . ."[12] The committee appointed a four-member subcommittee of legal experts, who decided that "the University of Toronto not only has the right, but the imperative duty to include in the curriculum of Arts the religious and theological subjects mentioned in the Section [129]. . . . Instruction is to be given in University College in the subjects named and in such other subjects as may from time to time be determined by statute. . . ." The committee's conclusions were that Blake's charges were "not well founded," but it added as a *douceur*, "Your Committee recognizes it as fundamental that teachers in University College must not trespass upon the field of Theology, and recommends that the Board of Governors, through the President, direct them accordingly."[13]

The work of McCurdy had thus been exonerated at the very time that President Falconer was representing the university at the Darwin centennial celebrations in Cambridge. Blake, however, had not been placated or silenced. He replied in a letter dated 15 January 1910 (printed as a thirteen-page pamphlet) that the committee had confused the issues. He was satisfied with its conclusion that University College was not in a position of equality with Victoria or Trinity, that the "objectionable" texts about which he complained had been ordered removed from use. The committee, however, had refused to be drawn into any discussion of what constituted "the orthodox position connected with the Bible," which did not reassure Blake.

[11] *Report of Special Committee to the Board of Governors, the University of Toronto, adopted 20th December, 1909* (Toronto: The University Press, n.d.) p. 4.
[12] WCA, O'Meara Papers, General Correspondence, 1907–10, S. H. Blake to T. R. O'Meara, 24 July 1909.
[13] *Report of Special Committee*, pp. 14, 8.

Theology had been too narrowly defined in the opinion of "all friends of the Bible." Students now boasted publicly "of their acceptance of the new teaching" and professors of biblical studies admitted that they belonged to "the new school." Further, these students were the very men and women destined to be ministers and teachers! "The authority of the Book has been greatly impaired," and "the national life and conscience is most deeply affected. . . . This result is not fair to those who entrust their young to the care of the Provincial University. They have a right to complain and continue to agitate, if in the most serious matter in the life and welfare of their children faith be not kept with them."[14] Better the Bible be withdrawn from the university curriculum than be left as "the sport of the University higher critic . . . thus creating an atmosphere in which it is dangerous for a Christian pupil to dwell." These were Blake's last words on the issue (he had just resigned as a governor of the university), but it was not the last time that the biblical scholars of the University of Toronto would come under attack for their disturbing theories. On the one side was ranged the claim of absolute certainty founded on faith, on the other freedom of inquiry, which might be destructive of beloved and believed preconceptions.

Higher Critics under Attack

If Blake's challenge to McCurdy's department and its teaching was an only slightly veiled attack on liberalism, three instances involving church-related colleges during the first decade of the century were clear-cut attempts to end the teaching of higher criticism and restore the primacy of biblical inerrancy as part of Christian orthodoxy. The first two occurred in Methodist colleges, and besides the issues of higher criticism and possible heresy each involved the Reverend Albert Carman, a pugnacious septuagenarian, general superintendent of the Methodist church since 1883, and a sworn enemy of change. For conservatives such as Carman the dangers of higher criticism had been brought home forcefully in 1906 by an episode that began in London, Ontario. The Methodist young people's Epworth League was sponsoring institutes of Old and New Testament literature and history which attracted large numbers of youthful Sunday school teachers to hear a team of experts lecture in favor of modernism and moral relativism. The impact of this teaching on an older generation was, however, cataclysmic: strong clergy and older adults literally blanched at the doctrines propounded and called on Carman to stop the sacrilege. "I believe," wrote one prominent matron, "Dr. Burwash, more than any other man in this Dominion, is responsible for the Unitarianism and the sceptic notions that are flooding the Methodist ministry." She was convinced that these individuals were more extreme than George C.

[14] *Mr. Blake's Acknowledgement of the Report of "The Board of Governors" on "The Teaching of Religious Knowledge in University College ult-a vires" and Other Matters* (Toronto: L. S. Haynes [1910]) pp. 9, 10, 12.

Workman: "It has become a sort of fad—a pretense of scholarship—"
another Methodist told Carman, "to parade radical ideas."[15] When Carman
challenged their teaching, the accused were quite unrepentant.

The first of the two cases involved Wesleyan Theological College in
Montreal, where W. J. Shaw had returned to the post of principal in 1901
and to his teaching in New Testament. James Cooper Antliffe, D.D., an
Englishman who had covered Hebrew and Old Testament studies on a part-
time basis since 1889, resigned that year, but three years passed before a
replacement was hired. His replacement was none other than George Workman, whose teaching had caused such a crisis at Victoria College thirteen
years earlier and whose appointment to Wesleyan is difficult to explain in
the light of his reputation and of the events that followed. Since his sudden
and dramatic departure from Victoria, Workman, a bachelor, had pursued
"private studies" and had published three books—*The Old Testament
Vindicated* (1897), *The Messianic Prophecy Vindicated* (1899), and *How to
Study the Bible* (1902)—and Shaw had described the first as "an excellent
antidote" to destructive higher criticism.

Apparently friction quickly developed over Workman's teaching and
caused divisions among students, faculty, and board members. Workman
was completing his third year at the college when Shaw, then in his sixty-
seventh year, appeared before the governors in April 1907 to charge Workman with having denied inherited depravity, the virgin birth, and the
historicity of the Fourth Gospel. By a vote of thirteen to nine the governors
resolved to investigate Shaw's accusations. One week later Workman laid a
complaint of libel against the principal on the basis of written accusations
given him by Shaw. Shaw in turn denied that he had any "malicious intent"
and claimed to be "keenly" hurt by this action of a colleague. After a
2½-day investigation by the Methodist district conference, Shaw was found
not guilty of libel.

With Workman's counteraction thus silenced, Shaw returned to his
primary purpose. Workman's teaching, he insisted, was heretical even if it
was "in good faith." Workman, he charged, was trying to put biblical
authority above his church's standards, and it was the college board's
responsibility to fire him.[16] The board criticized Workman's doctrinal position rather than his teaching, and a petition in his defense signed by thirty-
six students was first ignored by the board and then destroyed by its
secretary. The war of words continued with Workman appealing, on
grounds of improper procedure, the district conference's judgment in the

[15] UChA, Carman Papers, Box 18, file 123, M. R. Thornley to T. C. Scott, 23 February 1906;
ibid.. T. C. Scott to Albert Carman, 28 February 1906.
[16] UChA-MOC, M/57/1, broadsheet from Principal W. J. Shaw to governors and members of
the senate of Wesleyan Theological College, 16 May 1907, with handwritten notation, "For any
student who has had incorrect information as to the following & only for such."

libel matter, first to Albert Carman and then to the Quebec Superior Court in Montreal.[17] The civil court found in Workman's favor and ordered the college to pay costs and thirty-five hundred dollars damages, but on appeal this verdict was overturned on the grounds that secular courts had no authority over church courts in matters of belief and discipline. This decision was hailed rapturously by one of Carman's correspondents: "Boards can now dismiss professors for wrong teaching simply as a business proposition."[18]

That the college board was deeply divided throughout was apparent in a six-page "Personal Vindication" issued by Shaw, who stated that even though a minority of the governors was acting secretly to "damage" him, he personally would be "patient and forgiving."[19] More than a year after Shaw's original charges and after Workman had in fact left the college in 1908, Workman issued a twenty-eight-page rebuttal stating that Shaw was trying to shift the blame for his dismissal on to the board. This pamphlet closed with a letter to Workman from his friend and patron of Cobourg days, Principal Nathaniel Burwash, who summarized Workman's position neatly—the church would be in error "if she attempted to limit honest and devout investigation."[20] The same year, 1907, that he was removed from Wesleyan Theological College, George C. Workman published *The Servant of Jehovah*, a title with wry, if unintentional, undertones.

The second Methodist *cause célèbre* involved Carman, Burwash, and ultimately Victoria College. George Jackson, an English Wesleyan Methodist who had come to Toronto as a preacher in Sherbourne Street Church in 1906, had accepted in 1908 the additional appointment as professor of English Bible at Victoria, effective in 1909. A public lecture by Jackson to the Toronto Y.M.C.A. early in 1909 on the higher critics' interpretation of Genesis revived specifically many of the issues that had hovered around the Workman case. In the columns of the Toronto *Globe* of 26 February 1909 (rather than in the Methodists' *Christian Guardian*), Carman, who had neither seen Jackson's text nor communicated with him, denounced Jackson for "startling the uninstructed youth . . . by attacking the historicity of Holy Writ on points absolutely unassailable . . . thus loosening moral bonds, debauching the public mind and producing . . . doubters. . . ."

The ensuing controversy raged through the length of the Methodist church—in Winnipeg young clergy supported Jackson from the pulpit and a public sympathy meeting was called.[21] The principal of Alma Ladies

[17] Ibid., M/57/3, "Statement of Rev. Dr. Workman . . . Sept. 17th, 1907," 17 pages.

[18] UChA, Carman Papers, Box 16, file 106, J. S. Ross to Albert Carman, 6 February 1913.

[19] UChA-MOC, M/57/4, W. J. Shaw, "A Personal Vindication," ca. January 1908, 6 pages; UChA, Carman Papers, Box 20, file 133b, William Jackson to Albert Carman, 1 April 1908.

[20] UChA-MOC, M/57/5, "A Supplementary Statement" by G. C. Workman, 22 May 1908, 28 pages.

[21] UChA, Carman Papers, Box 13, file 82, Henry Kenner to Albert Carman, 25 March 1909.

College reported that all older Methodists supported Carman.[22] Already
Carman had sent a second letter to the *Globe*, printed on 12 March,
accusing Jackson in rough language of abusing Canadian Methodist hospitality and defending his own involvement. Carman had been compared with a
dogmatic medieval pope—"Dogmatic! and why not? I grew up in a dogmatic age and among a dogmatic people. We demand facts, and build our
business and our religion on facts and not on theories, fancies and illusions.
It is dogmatism all around me." Carman's struggle was no longer simply a
Methodist matter—it had become ecumenical. S. H. Blake, Anglican, welcomed Carman's suggestion for a meeting of common minds with Elmore
Harris, Baptist, and Dr. W. H. Hincks, Methodist, to form a permanent
organization to fight back years of insidious undermining and "to get rid of
our false Professors."[23] Both Blake and Carman soon produced pamphlets on
higher criticism, and Blake declared Carman's efforts had "a splendid
ring."[24]

After a month of public debate in the press, Jackson, Carman (who was
chairman of Victoria's board of regents), and every member of the college
faculty had signed a document in March supposedly resolving their differences by extracting a promise from Jackson not to publicize his biblical
views. In angry letters to Burwash, however, Carman accused Jackson one
month later of breaking their "amicable" agreement and of practicing the
duplicity so natural to higher critics. The question of Jackson's teaching was
brought before the Methodist church quadrennial conference in 1910
where, ironically, Carman and Burwash were billeted together. There one
of Jackson's conservative evangelical accusers stated, "As the higher critics
teach about Him He is no Savior at all. These higher critics base their
arguments on baseless assumptions. Their teachings are shipwrecking the
faith of hundreds."[25] By resolution the conference affirmed its adherence to
the word of God and acknowledged God as the infallible teacher, thus
circumventing the distinction between inerrant and infallible and shifting
the notion of infallibility away from the Bible. Control of the professors was
effectively left to the colleges, and since Victoria took no action against
Jackson he continued to teach there until 1913, when he returned to
England.

Among Baptists the issue of higher criticism emerged after the turn of
the century and remained active for a generation because the earlier confrontations produced neither a resolution nor even a workable modus
vivendi between liberals and conservatives. The controversy began around

[22] Ibid., R. I. Warner to Albert Carman, 19 March 1909.
[23] Ibid., S. H. Blake to Albert Carman, 30 April 1909.
[24] Ibid., Blake to Carman, 12 June 1909.
[25] Quoted in Tom Sinclair-Faulkner, "Theory Divided from Practice: The Introduction of the
Higher Criticism into Canadian Protestant Seminaries," *Canadian Society of Church History,
Papers 1979*, p. 51.

Isaac George Matthews, professor of Hebrew at McMaster University and generally regarded as representative of the growing influence of the University of Chicago on Canadian biblical studies. Ontario-born and a graduate of McMaster, Matthews had been hired in 1904 on completion of his theological course to replace the conservative Calvin Goodspeed in teaching systematic theology, Hebrew, Aramaic, and Old Testament exegesis. The source of the troubles at McMaster actually was George Cross, another of its graduates, who received a Chicago Ph.D. in 1899 and began teaching church history at McMaster in 1901. It was largely Cross's presence at McMaster that had led Matthews to accept a position there.

Spearheading the fundamentalist Baptist opposition to modernism was Elmore Harris, the friend of S. H. Blake and Albert Carman, senator and member of the board of McMaster University. Harris began accusing Matthews of a lack of spirituality, but the grounds for suspicion became an academic matter when Matthews was allowed eighteen months' leave to study at Chicago. This development was like a red flag to those who believed Chicago spawned heresy.[26] Probably this concern was heightened by curricular changes that tripled the time allotted to biblical studies in McMaster's theology program after 1905.[27] By 1908 Harris could no longer keep silent—he accused Matthews before the McMaster senate of teaching unorthodoxy. A year later Harris was in full pursuit of Matthews and Cross in a declared war à l'outrance. Cross in fact may have been the real quarry, but he had already accepted a post at Chicago so that the widespread ground swell of Baptist opinion against McMaster 'modernism" was concentrated on Matthews, the supposed "Babyloniophile."

Harris laid his charges against Matthews before the senate formally in May 1909—his evidence was lecture notes made by Matthews's students. A senate committee pronounced Matthews not guilty and added its own academic credo for public consumption. "McMaster University stands for freedom, for progress, for investigation. . . . Baptists have ever been ready to accord to all students of the Sacred Scriptures the largest possible measure of freedom consistent with loyalty to the fundamentals of the Christian faith."[28] Harris was not silenced by this statement but was stimulated to retort that Matthews as an individual "can hold all the vagaries of the Higher Critics he pleases," but those opinions must not be voiced ex cathedra in the theological department. As in the Workman case, the issue was simply that whoever paid the theological professor must by right determine the theological tune played to the students.

[26] C. M. Johnston, McMaster University Volume 1/The Toronto Years (Toronto: University of Toronto Press, 1976) pp. 92ff.

[27] Canadian Baptist, 23 February 1905.

[28] Quoted in Johnston, McMaster University Volume 1, p. 105.

Matthews answered Harris's printed word with printed word. "It is not sufficient that [the] teacher possess exact knowledge of the past only . . . he must be able also to reinterpret the message in terms of the present."[29] "In the years following 1910 Matthews took pains not to abuse his prerogative as a teacher and to present controversial concepts more chastely."[30] Nevertheless, the issue continued to simmer in Baptist circles, and even the sudden death of Harris in 1911 did not stop the growing rift. He had acquired a friend and worthy successor in the person of Thomas Todhunter Shields of Jarvis Street Church in Toronto, who would revive the denominational struggle over modernist influences a dozen years later when the unsettling effects of World War I created a new sense of urgency in the matter.

"From this point on, higher criticism was taught without formal challenge in the Methodist seminaries of Canada,"[31] Tom Sinclair-Faulkner has written of the Jackson case. "The higher critics were safe, at least in the lecture halls." In Canadian Methodist circles higher criticism was tolerated because "those who sought peace achieved it by defining the work of the higher critics as theory, abstractions to be considered apart from that which is 'really' important: the practice of piety." "George Jackson," he concludes,

> was a higher critic who consistently strove to read the Bible with "awe" as he put it, studying the Scriptures for themselves, not only as a tool for better living. Though rooted in the modern age he attempted to do both *theoria* and *praxis* and to unite them harmoniously in his work as a seminary professor. He was not altogether successful, in general because of the modern tendency to denigrate theory and thus to divide it from practice, in particular because of the Methodist decisions of 1909–10 that exacerbated this tendency among Canadian Protestants.

A Successor for McCurdy

Scarcely had Blake's attack on the Department of Orientals been repulsed in 1910 before a new and more prolonged drama regarding personnel began to unfold for McCurdy and the University of Toronto. In February, McCurdy informed President Falconer that he had been invited to fill the prestigious post of annual director for the American School of Oriental Research in Jerusalem during 1911–12. Charles C. Torrey had written that McCurdy's involvement in the school would be good for the University of Toronto and for biblical studies in Canada. McCurdy asked for leave of absence with salary but offered to pay for a replacement and to supervise

---

[29] Quoted ibid., pp. 107–8.

[30] C. H. Pinnock, "The Modernist Impulse at McMaster University, 1887–1927," in *Baptists in Canada*, ed. J. K. Zeman (Burlington, Ont.: G. R. Welch, 1980) p. 199.

[31] Sinclair-Faulkner, "Theory Divided from Practice," p. 52. This conclusion was voiced at Victoria College's centennial celebrations in 1936. See *On the Old Ontario Strand: Victoria's Hundred Years* (Toronto: Victoria University, 1936) p. 143.

the work of any Toronto graduate students studying in Jerusalem.[32] His absence was going to be complicated by Richard Davidson's resignation in 1910.

While McCurdy was in Berlin en route to the Holy Land he wrote to Falconer reciting the development of Orientals at Toronto and outlining his plans for future development. Before 1886 "scarcely anything more than a little Hebrew was taught in the Old University College . . . and that for the purpose of meeting the need of theological students." Since his arrival, however,

> the scope of the curriculum has broadened in conformity with the widening conception of the relations of the Bible to human history and of its necessary place in the development of our civilization. Accordingly the study of the language, literature and history of Israel has always occupied at least half of the time given to Semitics in lectures and class work as a whole . . . We shall, I am sure, develop the studies cognate with Hebrew, duly enlarge our library, and establish at length a more than creditable museum; but I think the time will never come when our interest in these matters from the purely scientific side will be greater than our devotion to the elucidation and illustration of the Bible.

This philosophy, McCurdy believed, should govern the choice of future additions to the faculty. Any head of the department must serve "the primary claim" of the theological schools as well as scientific biblical studies.

> Ontario, though perhaps the most cultured part of Canada, is as yet a new country and demands almost exclusively the learning which is supposed to yield practical results. . . . Men of like culture and love of science, with a thorough linguistic archeological and historical training would best educate the students into a true appreciation of Oriental knowledge by setting the whole subject before them in its right relation, and would in the end make of them better scholars and teachers.

Because each federated college had "its own traditional claims and susceptibilities," caution and prudence must be observed in the work of the department. New appointees to faculty should know and understand these facts.[33] McCurdy had also decided, as a result of his visits in Eruope, that a European scholar would not enjoy working with Canadian undergraduates whose maturing seemed slower than that of European students. American academic experience suggested that the best teachers were "native-bred men with good foreign training superadded to their home education. . . . The evils of inbreeding are minimized in these later days by the cosmopolitan character of science and of the higher education; and in such a department as that of Semitics it is scarcely to be expected that they would emerge at all." McCurdy closed his long agenda for his department by saying that he was reading Arabic and Assyrian and enjoying the lectures of his old friend and teacher, the younger Delitzsch, and of Eduard Meyer.

---

[32] UTA, Falconer Papers, Box 10, J. F. McCurdy to Sir R. A. Falconer, 3 February 1910, and enclosure.

[33] Ibid., Box 20, J. F. McCurdy to Sir R. A. Falconer, 10 June 1911.

Eleven days later Falconer asked William Robert Taylor if he would be a special lecturer in the Department of Orientals for the coming winter.[34] Taylor, a native son of Ontario, had graduated with first class honors in Orientals under McCurdy from University College in 1904, proceeded to Knox College—and J. E. McFadyen—for theology, and then pursued graduate studies at the University of Toronto, receiving both the M.A. and Ph.D. in 1910. His doctoral thesis, entitled "The Originality of the Hebrew Text of Ben Sira in the Light of the Vocabulary and the Version," had been completed under McCurdy. In McCurdy's estimation Taylor was such a good teacher, scholar, and person, already competent in Hebrew and so well grounded in Aramaic and Assyrian, that with a year or so abroad he "would take a good place among the Semitists of America."[35] When Falconer wrote to Taylor the latter was returning to Canada from a year's study in Berlin, and having just accepted a professorship at Westminster Hall, the new Presbyterian seminary in Vancouver, he could get only a year's release.

Falconer felt "it would be a pity to take him [Taylor] from British Columbia, where at this time of our country's growth, there is need of the strongest type of man for the upbuilding of a young country."[36] Besides, "it would be an unwise step on our part to appoint a Presbyterian to this post"—Falconer, McCurdy, Davidson, McRae, and Eakin were all Presbyterians (as Murison and McGee had been too), and all but Falconer and McCurdy were graduates of Knox College! Falconer believed "a graduate of another University would strengthen our staff." His preference was a well-recommended Cambridge scholar, Herbert Loewe, "a very devout Jew" and "a very good Arabist." "It is true," he added, "that it would be unwise to have any but a professing Christian at the head of the Oriental Department, and Mr. Loewe would not necessarily ever occupy that position." Falconer intended to consult Davidson and McLaughlin to get the views of the federated colleges on his proposal.

McCurdy responded that he personally could not support Loewe for the position because of Loewe's restricted area of academic work and because the affiliated colleges might resent the promotion of a Jew. He closed this letter with another problem for Falconer—because of his age and failing eyesight McCurdy wanted to find someone who could replace himself as chairman of Orientals within a very few years.[37] Again Falconer wrote, early in January 1912, urging Loewe's appointment as professor of Arabic. Neither Principal Alfred Gandier of Knox nor Principal O'Meara of Wycliffe objected to the appointment of a Jew, but a week later McCurdy's letter reached Falconer. The latter now replied that as far as Loewe was concerned, he did not wish "to

[34] Ibid., Box 15, Sir R. A. Falconer to W. R. Taylor, 21 June 1911.
[35] Ibid., Box 26, J. F. McCurdy to Sir R. A. Falconer, 23 August 1911.
[36] Ibid., Box 19, Sir R. A. Falconer to J. F. McCurdy, 19 September 1911.
[37] Ibid., Box 26, J. F. McCurdy to Sir R. A. Falconer, 26 December 1911.

force upon you any conditions, which would in your judgment interfere with a department which is in the main your own creation, and the spirit of which you understand as no one else does." As for McCurdy's proposed retirement he added, "Perhaps you may have found someone during your visit abroad who will appeal to you as being likely to fill the chair."[38]

At this point Austin Perley Misener, the popular young professor of Oriental languages at Victoria College (where he had begun teaching in 1900 before going to Leipzig in 1907), died at the age of thirty-nine after severe and prolonged suffering. To fill this gap William Arthur Potter, a graduate of 1900, was called back temporarily, although his appointment was soon made permanent. Falconer advised McCurdy of possible personnel problems arising from Misener's death, but meanwhile Loewe had arrived at the school in Jerusalem early in the new year. McCurdy reported to the president after a three-weeks' acquaintance with the young Jew that, erudite as he was, he put the New Testament in the same class as the Koran! He also seemed to be involved in Zionism, and McCurdy decided he was too dangerous to be appointed to the University of Toronto.[39] He recommended Taylor instead, but Taylor had found the inducements at Toronto too small.

At the end of June, McCurdy dispatched a twelve-page letter to Falconer from Paris about a new candidate. Immanuel G. A. Benzinger was forty-six years old, a product of the University of Berlin and licentiate of the Evangelical Lutheran Church. He had published extensively and had lived in Palestine for the past decade. He taught Hebrew and German in a secondary school for thirty-four hours each week, acted as Dutch Vice-Consul, and operated a travel agency promoting tours of Egypt and the Holy Land. Benzinger knew many ancient and modern languages and spoke English well. McCurdy had asked Benzinger if he would be interested in an appointment, and he had replied affirmatively.

Falconer, who had arrived in London, had heard criticisms of Benzinger's writings which he repeated to McCurdy. McCurdy responded that such criticisms were not unfair but were undiscriminating. Benzinger was not a "Pan-Babylonist" nor guilty of "one-sided Wincklerianism," a reference to Hugo Winckler's assertion of a unity of Near Eastern culture derived from Babylonian cosmography, which Friedrich Delitzsch expanded into the "Bible versus Babel" controversy by further exaggerating this indebtedness to Babylon. McCurdy was convinced also that Benzinger's business interests would not interfere with his teaching. Despite his heavy undertakings he still wrote more than many leisured scholars. Indeed, his German training would be "a good example for those of Canadian training who in educational matters are apt to take principles and methods for granted." However, Benzinger would not go to Toronto for a trial year because of his business.

[38] Ibid., Box 19, Sir R. A. Falconer to J. F. McCurdy, 17 January 1912.
[39] Ibid., Box 26, J. F. McCurdy to Sir R. A. Falconer, 11 February 1912.

McCurdy was insistent that a permanent appointment be made. He must soon retire from the chairmanship and therefore "a worthy incumbent" to be his successor should be trained now, "at this present critical moment."[40] Richard Davidson, then of Knox, who had joined the McCurdys in Paris, was sure Benzinger was such a scholar as "would adorn our department among North American Universities."

Falconer wrote back indicating further reservations about the negotiations with Benzinger. Davidson and McCurdy read his letter and "were quite puzzled and perplexed." Benzinger had already telegraphed to McCurdy that he was prepared to come to Toronto in October, and since he had to dispose of his travel agency, McCurdy felt there was a moral obligation to compensate him if he did not get the appointment. The chairman was convinced that the University of Toronto could not afford to miss the chance of getting Benzinger on its faculty. For five years McCurdy had carried both pass and honors work in Orientals singlehandedly, and of those whom he enlisted as assistants (McGee and Murison died, Davidson and Taylor left) only Thomas Eakin remained—and his work was limited to undergraduate teaching at University College.

McCurdy felt the department was "threatened with deterioration" and that he had only a short time left to "strengthen the things that remain." Benzinger was "a veritable Godsend in the literal sense of the term," who could sustain the two objectives of the department, namely, to make Hebrew literature the center of the curriculum and to offer the language, literature, and history of other Semitic peoples. Benzinger's work had been praised by R. Kittel, a further proof of his scholarship. To Falconer's somewhat sarcastic comment that so distinguished a scholar would have to be made head of the department, McCurdy replied in kind, "I should not like to think that any man was too good for Toronto University."[41]

Opinions from six international scholars, however, cast further doubt on Benzinger's suitability. One said that his theological views would be more "advanced" than Falconer might wish. The president asserted that he had never feared frank biblical criticism, but "if we are not to injure the Oriental Department we must go carefully just now." The board of governors had been "broad minded" and had recognized the department as "legitimate" (presumably a reference to Blake's charges), but the president did not want "unnecessary criticism." Three of the scholars consulted had asked why Benzinger had quit the University of Berlin.[42] McCurdy had an answer—a man who disliked Benzinger said he had left Berlin because of scandal involving a friend's wife, but a university-authorized investigation

[40] Ibid., Box 26, Richard Davidson to Sir R. A. Falconer, 18 July 1912; Box 24, J. F. McCurdy to Sir R. A. Falconer, 17 July 1912.
[41] Ibid., Box 24, J. F. McCurdy to Sir R. A. Falconer, 24 July 1912.
[42] Ibid., Sir R. A. Falconer to J. F. McCurdy, 29 July 1912, copy.

had found Benzinger innocent and had offered him his job again.[43] In due course Benzinger received the Toronto appointment and assumed his teaching duties in the autumn of 1912 (just as Thomas Eakin resigned to enter law studies), but the Toronto *News* reported on 18 December 1912 that Benzinger had only two students and the whole of the Orientals department only fourteen! Taylor finally agreed to join the staff in 1913, and McCurdy resigned in the spring of 1914. Immediately Taylor was promoted from special lecturer to professor, and Benzinger became chairman of the department. Prospects for the department looked good as the university term ended in the spring of 1914, but before a new academic year commenced western civilization was plunged into World War I.

When Canada entered the war on 4 August as part of the British empire, Benzinger was visiting in Germany. He managed to return through Rotterdam and arrived in Toronto early in October.[44] Falconer had already written to the Canadian government expressing his hope that no problems would arise because of Benzinger's citizenship,[45] but before the end of December, as anti-German feelings swept the Canadian public, Benzinger resigned. The board of governors responded generously by placing him on leave with pay for the remainder of the session, and Falconer, regretting this crippling loss to the department, voiced the high regard of faculty and students for Benzinger's ability and for his neutrality "during this testing crisis."[46] Already the press and some of the university governors had called for the dismissal of four German-born professors, a demand resolutely resisted by Falconer. For this "unpatriotic" stance the University of Toronto was denounced as being pro-German. On 7 December the Toronto *Telegram* printed Benzinger's picture over the caption, "Another of the German University professors whose pay will go on, although they have been given leave of absence." McCurdy himself fanned such antagonism by refusing to stand when "God Save the King" was sung during the Sunday service at St. Andrew's Presbyterian Church.[47] McCurdy was by conviction a pacifist, an acknowledged admirer of German culture and scholarship, and furthermore, Benzinger was at that moment his house guest!

Worse was still to come for the refugee professor whose son was seriously wounded while serving on the eastern front. Under an order-in-council of 15 August enemy aliens were to be interned for the duration, but Benzinger was given permission on 21 January to leave Canada within twelve days and avoid prison. Twenty-four hours later he departed by train for Princeton.[48] His connection with the university had been brief and

[43] Ibid., J. F. McCurdy to Sir R. A. Falconer, 1 August 1912.
[44] Ibid., Box 33, I. G. A. Benzinger to Sir R. A. Falconer, 19 September 1914.
[45] Ibid., Sir R. A. Falconer to ?, 25 September 1914.
[46] Ibid., Sir R. A. Falconer to I. G. A. Benzinger, 31 December 1914.
[47] *Telegram*, 21 December 1914.
[48] *Mail* 22 January 1915; *Star*, 22 January 1915.

troubled, but this was not his last contact with the institution. In 1923 he got a letter of reference from Falconer when applying for a post at the University of Riga. Three years later he showed his appreciation by sending Falconer his latest publication, a three-volume work of edited papers.[49] The episode of Benzinger and the other three German professors was not quickly forgotten nor forgiven by other Canadians. Two years later a writer in *Saturday Night* commented, "The President has never shown much independence save in his notion that German professors ought to be kept on the payroll of Toronto University even if our country is at war with the Hun."[50]

Scholars Old and New

In the generation before World War I the unique developments at Toronto—the federation of secular and church-related universities and the creation of a strong department of Oriental languages within a nondenominational ("godless") institution—certainly meant that biblical studies there outstripped achievements elsewhere in Canada, both quantitatively and qualitatively. Nevertheless the growing interest in biblical studies as a legitimate and discrete academic discipline was reflected in the appointments of specialists at several institutions and in the wider offering of biblical literature courses at the undergraduate level, even if no full departments for such studies were created.

With the departure of George Jackson from Victoria College in 1913 the board of regents for the first time hired faculty directly from Great Britain. Welsh-born John Hugh Michael, impressive in appearance and speech, became associate professor of New Testament exegesis. "In the classroom his emphasis on jot and tittle proved tedious to some of the young brethren who preferred to take the Kingdom by banalities."[51] Off campus Michael was an active supporter of the Toronto Eisteddfod. A mild conservative and quiet evangelical, Michael proved to be a good choice on the part of Chairman John F. McLaughlin, who, if he personally made evident his own "sympathy with the higher critics,"[52] was nonetheless aware of the need for gradualism regarding the teaching of higher criticism in Methodist colleges. The second associate professor appointed to Orientals at Victoria in 1913, Samuel H. Hooke, was a less fortunate choice. An Oxford graduate in theology and Semitic languages and an exceptional all-round athlete, "Sammy" Hooke had won a number of scholarships and had served a decade

[49] UTA, Falconer Papers, Box 76, letters of reference, 11 February, 7 March 1923; Box 92, Sir R. A. Falconer to I. G. A. Benzinger, 7 May 1926.

[50] *Saturday Night*, 4 December 1916.

[51] C. B. Sissons, *A History of Victoria University* (Toronto: University of Toronto Press, 1952) p. 263.

[52] *Globe*, 23 September 1909.

on the staff of England's largest theological correspondence school. There was no question of his ability as a scholar and little doubt of his ability as a teacher, but time was to show how insensitive Hooke could be to conservative Canadian habits of mind.

Trinity College, now settled at its new home on the University of Toronto campus, within sight of Wycliffe, Victoria, and University colleges, was still plagued by frequent changes of junior personnel in the field of biblical studies and by the administrative and ecclesiastical demands placed on senior faculty. Henry Thomas Duckworth, an Oxford graduate who had published popular histories about the Near East, came in 1901 and among other subjects taught biblical literature until his death in 1927. In 1907 the college acquired one of the major figures in its history and a highly respected biblical scholar. Francis ("Frank") Herbert Cosgrave was a graduate of Trinity College Dublin, just twenty-four years old when he was appointed to Trinity in Toronto. At his retirement thirty-eight years later he had served the college as lecturer, professor, dean of theology, and provost and had received five honorary degrees from Canadian universities. Cosgrave taught both Old and New Testament in his early days at Trinity, and if the heavy burden of the provostship circumscribed his own opportunities for research and publication, at least his office made it possible for him in time to seek, acquire, and encourage as colleagues individuals who were biblical scholars of renown.

At Wycliffe College, facing the Oxfordian spires of the new Trinity building across Hoskin Avenue, Principal Sheraton still carried the burden of teaching (with some assistance from nearby parish clergy) until 1905 when Thomas Herbert Cotton became librarian and professor of apologetics and Old Testament. Sheraton died in harness in 1906, his thirtieth year as principal, and was succeeded by Thomas Robert O'Meara. That same year Charles Venn Pilcher, Oxford graduate and scion of a famous Evangelical family, arrived to teach New Testament. Unfortunately, in 1908 Pilcher became the center of an incident erroneously assumed to have arisen from some "modernistic" tendencies in his teaching. A shy, awkward, innocent, and donnish person, Pilcher quit the college almost without notice but for reasons unconnected with biblical studies. On the eve of his wedding, student wags painted on his luggage graffiti that he believed reflected on his honor and that of his fiancée. Unable to cope with this emotional crisis, Pilcher resigned his professorship, applied large quantities of paint remover to the offending messages, and departed with one-way tickets for England on his honeymoon.[53]

As for Knox College, its historically close relationship to University

---

[53] T. R. Millman, "To Charles Venn Pilcher, in grateful memory," *Cap and Gown* 39 (1962) 57–62; WCA, O'Meara Papers, Personal Letters, April 1908, especially T. R. O'Meara to Mrs. Pilcher, 23 April 1908.

College was further strengthened after the turn of the century by the decision to abandon the old buildings on Spadina Avenue and to relocate, like Trinity, on the nearby university campus within a stone's throw of McCurdy's department. The old gothic structure of Knox was in need of costly repairs and a college committee was appointed in 1905 to report on "the merits and demerits of the proposal to change the site of the College, expecially [sic] from an ecclesiastical and educational point of view."[54] The new buildings did not open until 1915, but in that interval yet another bond between Knox and the university was forged—in 1908 Alfred Gandier, brother of President Falconer's wife, became Knox's fourth principal.

Knox, which supplied so many graduates to McCurdy's postgraduate program, lost J. E. McFadyen in 1910 when he returned to Scotland. During his twelve-year stay in Toronto he had published no fewer than nine books, including two on the psalms, one on the prophetic and historical scriptures, one entitled *Old Testament Criticism and the Christian Church* (1903) and another, *Introduction to the Old Testament* (1905). McFadyen's "liberalism" may not have pleased everyone, but his personal piety, reasonableness, and scholarship were never challenged. "He was," in the opinion of W. G. Jordan, "remarkable for his soberness of judgment, his patience and tact. . . . There is no man who had done more to present modern scholarship in clear, persuasive style to a large circle of readers in Canada, the United States and Britain."[55] His successor at Knox was Richard Davidson, McCurdy's friend and former student, while the college's first appointee in New Testament was H. A. A. Kennedy, a former classmate of Robert Falconer at Berlin. Kennedy arrived from Scotland in 1905 and departed for New College, Edinburgh, four years later, leaving no evidence of his influence. His replacement was another Scot, Robert Law, who had already achieved prominence as a preacher and author. Law had done postgraduate studies at Tübingen and was recommended for the Knox post by Dr. James Denney when the latter visited Toronto in 1909.[56] Law accepted the additional duty of ministering to Old St. Andrew's congregation in the city, and the double demands on his time reduced his scholarly production. Nevertheless he did publish two more books before his death in 1919, and one of these, *The Tests of Life* (1909), a classic study of the first epistle of St. John, was reprinted as recently as 1978.

At Queen's in Kingston, John B. Mowat was still teaching Hebrew at the close of the century at the age of seventy-four after forty-two undistinguished years in the professoriate. Mowat's unimportance as a biblical scholar was reflected in the lines of a contemporary college song, "Does you

[54] KCA, Committee on permanent site of College, draft minutes, 27 October 1905.
[55] W. G. Jordan, "The Higher Criticism in Canada. II. The Canadian Situation," *Queen's Quarterly* 36 (1929) 37–38.
[56] *The Presbyterian*, 16 September 1909, p. 259.

know the gentle Rabbi who makes the critics quail?/Does you know that he can demonstrate that Jonah ate the whale?" His pedagogical impact was recorded by one student: Mowat, "a kindly old man . . . would sit meditatively at our discussions, and if later on he owned that he had 'had his doubts about it at the time', he never troubled us by telling them."[57] In 1899 William George Jordan, a native of England, was given a Queen's D.D. and was designated as Mowat's successor. Commenting three decades later on the intellectual climate of Queen's at the turn of the century, the higher critic Jordan wrote, "On my first appearance at Queen's I found that the soil had been prepared and the atmosphere was quite genial. Principal [G. M.] Grant and Dr. [John] Watson were in sympathy with the new methods."[58]

A year before Jordan's appointment, Scottish-born E. F. Scott had been made professor of church history. As was the case with Jordan, Scott's considerable impact as a teacher and writer in the field of biblical studies was still ahead of him at this time—he produced four important monographs before World War I. The greatest change at Queen's, however, was not in personnel but in structure, because after more than a decade of discussion Queen's was secularized in 1910 and only its theological department retained a connection with the Presbyterian church. By that date both Jordan and Scott had begun to establish their reputations as biblical scholars. Between 1902 and 1916 Jordan produced no fewer than six books, while his colleague and friend won worldwide acclaim for his second volume, *The Fourth Gospel* (1908), as well as the sobriquet "Scott of the Fourth Gospel." In the considered opinion of his colleague Jordan, Scott's *Apologetic of the New Testament* (1907) and his *St. John's Gospel* (1911) had "placed him in the front rank of New Testament scholars."[59] Ironically, Scott's *Biblical Criticism and Modern Thought* was published in 1910, just after S. H. Blake's attack on the teaching of McCurdy's department at the University of Toronto.

At McGill, the development of biblical studies made little advance in the opening decades of the century. In 1907, the Reverend Charles Alexander Brodie Brockwell, a Yorkshireman who had graduated from Oxford and King's, Nova Scotia, and who defined himself as a "Christian Socialist," was appointed to teach biblical languages. Brockwell taught Hebrew until 1936, except for 1934–35 when he gave classes in law and history. His impact on biblical studies and even on McGill is unclear; there is no record of any major publication by him although he was proud to be known as the author of a poem, "Empire-Science-Faith." During the search

[57] T. R. Glover and D. D. Calvin, *A Corner of Empire: The Old Ontario Strand* (Cambridge: University Press, 1937) pp. 135–36.

[58] Jordan, "Higher Criticism," p. 38; see also W. L. Grant and F. Hamilton, *Principal Grant* (Toronto: Morang, 1904) pp. 490ff.

[59] Jordan, "Higher Criticism," p. 44.

for a successor to McCurdy he let it be known that he was interested in the chairmanship at Toronto because McGill's lack of funds "restrain my natural ambitions." But President Falconer had already decided that Brockwell was "unlikely [to] . . . suit the position in every respect."[60]

One development with positive long-term implications for biblical studies at McGill was the launching in 1912 of a scheme for cooperative theological education by the four affiliated theological colleges—Congregational, Diocesan, Wesleyan, and Presbyterian. This scheme was largely the brainchild of William Massey Birks, a wealthy Montreal jeweler who raised over a half million dollars to provide a "neutral" building to supplement the facilities of the four cooperating colleges. A joint curriculum was established for the academic year 1912–13 and a year later "The Joint Board of the Theological Colleges Affiliated with McGill University" was incorporated by statute. Denominational history and church polity were taught separately by each college, and to counter high church Anglican opposition to interdenominational cooperation Diocesan College also reserved to itself several other subjects, including New Testament exegesis.

Within the cooperating colleges there were a number of changes in personnel teaching biblical studies. Workman's replacement at Wesleyan Theological College was Walter Melville Patton, a graduate of McGill, Wesleyan, Yale, and Heidelberg, who had previously spent five years teaching at the college. He returned from a successful teaching career in the United States in 1908, and at Shaw's death three years later he became principal of the college. Patton, however, remained only one year after the formation of the joint board before moving back to the United States permanently. Diocesan Theological had G. Abbott-Smith, Steen's successor, in its biblical studies department, and Presbyterian College could contribute the ripe scholarship of John Scrimger to the consortium. Congregational College appointed Harlan Creelman as its professor of Hebrew in 1899. Creelman had gone from the University of New Brunswick to Yale's graduate school, where he had become an instructor in Hebrew. After nine years at Congregational College he returned to the United States to take a post at Auburn Theological Seminary. His successor was Scottish-born and educated Alexander Reid Gordon, who had studied at Freiburg, Göttingen, and Berlin, had published *The Early Tradition of Genesis* (1907)—a book highly commended by J. E. McFadyen—and who had spent the past two years teaching in Presbyterian College.

During this period there were few developments of importance in the field of biblical studies among other Canadian institutions. At Mount Allison University, C. H. Paisley was replaced in 1908 as professor of New Testament by Howard Sprague, one of the university's first graduates, while Charles Stewart was succeeded in Old Testament exegesis in 1903 by W. G.

60 UTA, Falconer Papers, Box 19, Sir R. A. Falconer to J. F. McCurdy, 17 January 1912.

Watson, a Victoria alumnus who had done postgraduate Hebrew studies with McCurdy. In 1901 Acadia hired Arthur Crawley Chute, one of its own students who had gone to Chicago for theological training as G. P. Payzant Professor of Hebrew Language and Biblical Literature, a chair Chute filled until 1922 although he apparently never published in the field of biblical studies. The condition of biblical studies was not much better at Huron College. There, Charles Cameron Waller, a Cambridge graduate who had also studied Hebrew at Bad Homburg, was appointed principal in 1902. He took over the teaching of Hebrew when S. E. G. Edelstein, a converted Polish Jew nicknamed "Yod" by his students, resigned about 1906 after fifteen years' service. In addition to his own chores in Bible, New Testament Greek, the Articles, Latin, the Prayer Book, Genesis, and Greek patristics, Waller carried the regular administrative duties of his office.

In western Canada, the older colleges that formed the University of Manitoba—Manitoba (Presbyterian), Wesley (Methodist), and St. John's (Anglican)—were joined in the new century by provincial universities in Saskatchewan, Alberta, and British Columbia; but only the older institutions were offering Old Testament language and literature at that time. At Manitoba College Scottish-born principal John Mark King represented the German tradition in biblical scholarship until his death in 1899. E. Perry Guthrie, an ardent athlete and graduate of the college, had been at both Berlin and Leipzig and was appointed to the chair of Old Testament in 1905, the year he received his Leipzig Ph.D. Two generations of students recalled Perry's practice of shouting his lectures. At the death of Principal King a memorial chair of New Testament had been established and its first incumbent was Principal William Patrick, better remembered as an initiator of church union in Canada.

Associated with Perry and with Andrew Browning Baird, Manitoba College's first appointee in Old Testament language and literature, was a part-time lecturer, Gilbert B. Wilson, a local minister who had graduated from Toronto, had studied in Berlin, and had earned his Ph.D. from Halle in 1900 while on a Knox College traveling fellowship. Wilson was the author of an item entitled "The Extent and Religious Value of the Psalter in use in the Temple of Solomon" and of a pamphlet in German on the dissolution of the English monasteries. At Wesley College Oriental languages and literature were offered from 1903 to 1913 by Salem Goldsworth Bland, a leading and controversial figure in the history of the social gospel in Canada. Bland's interpretation of scripture proved to be too advanced for some members of the Methodist church, and in an action reminiscent of the Jackson case one year earlier, Bland was formally accused in 1910 of teaching "unsound doctrine." The specific charges were that Bland had said St. Paul had made mistakes and that the serpent story was a myth. Unlike the Jackson case, however, Bland's difficulties came to a sudden and unexpected conclusion because popular opinion in Winnipeg was so strongly in his favor that no one could be found willing to serve on a trial committee![61]

On the national scene, the most notable change in biblical studies undoubtedly had been the departure of J. F. McCurdy, the father of the discipline in Canada. At McCurdy's retirement J. F. McLaughlin offered a perceptive assessment of McCurdy's contributions and influence on the development of the field during the previous three decades: "There is a deep felt sense of loss, amounting almost to bereavement, this year, in the department of Oriental Languages, owing to the absence of Dr. McCurdy from the place he has so long been accustomed to fill in class room and in council." McCurdy had created that undergraduate department, and as it grew he "found himself sought after by an increasing number of graduates, eager to continue their Semitic studies. Most of these men were candidates for the Christian ministry. With far sighted wisdom he realised the opportunity which was thus presented of building up a competent Biblical scholarship in Canada, which might compare, in some measure at least, with that which was the peculiar glory and strength of the churches of England and Scotland. Then, as though it were a matter of course, he set himself with self-sacrificing zeal to the task."[62]

McCurdy had developed in "godless" University College a four-year course on Hebrew literature and history comparable to the religious knowledge courses offered in the federated denominational colleges. From the beginning his classes were open to students of those other colleges who had come "to share with those of University College the same high regard and affectionate esteem for him as their master. In these more advanced classes . . . Dr. McCurdy was at his best. His wide knowledge, his thoroughness, his patience, his well-balanced judgment, never hasty, and singularly free from prejudice, won for him the confidence of his students, just as his unfailing courtesy, considerateness and kindness won their affectionate regard." McLaughlin believed McCurdy's greatest satisfaction must have come from the "honourable and useful service" of his students, some of whom had achieved international distinction as teachers and scholars.

At the personal level McLaughlin recalled how years earlier McCurdy had gathered his fellow scholars at his home for "conversation and study" in an atmosphere of "hospitality" and "kindly fellowship." "Our meetings became more frequent, and finally grew into the Biblical Club. . . . Dr. McCurdy was our first and has been our only president." McLaughlin's eulogy ended with an instructive comparison of McCurdy and his own teacher S. R. Driver.

> Both have exercised, by their wealth of knowledge, by their wide sympathies, by their moderation, and by their unaffected faith in the verities of religion, a steadying influence

[61] UChA, Carman Papers, Box 14, file 86, H. Kenner to Albert Carman, 18 February, 24 February, 23 April 1910.
[62] *University Monthly* 15 (1914–15) 204–8.

upon the thought of their time. Thirty years ago the historical and critical methods of Bible study, while not by any means unknown, had made but little progress in England or in Canada, and had scarcely more than obtained a foothold in British and American universities. Now all is changed and these methods are almost universally accepted. The fear of damaging results to faith is disappearing, and hostility is disarmed. Criticism has freed itself from some of its own earlier extravagances and follies, and is no longer looked upon as an instrument of unbelief. . . . It is only just to attribute to Dr. McCurdy the same kind of helpful influence in this University, and so in the thought of this country, as that exercised in so marked a way by Dr. Driver in Oxford.

In the first score of years in the twentieth century, biblical studies in Canada had indeed advanced substantially, both in qualitative and in quantitative terms. Although the University of Toronto, particularly University and Victoria colleges, had made the most notable progress in terms of curriculum and scholarship, appointments at other institutions did hold promise of future growth in the discipline. Outstanding teachers had graced the field in those years, and their record of publication, especially of monographs, was impressive for that period. The place of higher criticism within the academic program had been established despite some lingering popular suspicions. John W. Hart's comment that "American Modernism was not the radical liberalism [found] in Germany . . . [it] was both much younger in its development and more sympathetic to evangelical Christianity," is equally applicable to Canada.[63] A climate for "frank, scientific discussion" had been created, albeit within a tradition that emphasized a tactful or even conservative approach. Finally, in those two decades there had emerged a group of young scholars who were destined to play in the coming years a significant role in the expansion of biblical studies at both the national and the international level.

[63] J. W. Hart, "Princeton Theological Seminary: The Reorganization of 1929," *Journal of Presbyterian History* 58 (1980) 136.

III

MILDEWED WITH DISCRETION

The University is obsessed with a ruinous caution and . . . is mildewed with discretion.

William Andrew Irwin, 1930

Changes at Toronto

If World War I had any good results for biblical studies they were most obvious in the field of Near Eastern archeology. The freeing of much of the former Turkish Empire and the creation of Arab states allied to Britain by gratitude and self-interest made biblical archeology there possible on a scale hitherto unknown. Throughout the twenties and much of the thirties expeditions funded from Western countries, particularly from the United States, undertook digs whose findings had wide repercussions on biblical studies. In this development Canadian scholars played a prominent part, although usually as members of teams sponsored by non-Canadian institutions. A second result, more apparent in hindsight perhaps than in the immediate wake of the war, was a more liberal and open tone of life, reflected generally in the revolutionary social changes of the twenties but specifically in biblical studies by a popular readiness to accept or at least tolerate the kind of criticism that had involved Workman, Jackson, Steen, and even slightly McFadyen in controversy.

On the Toronto scene the first postwar incident involving a biblical scholar had little immediate reference to biblical studies but did have lasting results. To replace Benzinger the university had hired James Alexander Craig from McGill in 1915 over a number of well-known applicants. Craig, aged sixty-one, a graduate of McGill and Yale and proud owner of a Leipzig Ph.D., was an ordained Presbyterian minister. He had taught Old Testament at Oberlin Theological Seminary and at the University of Michigan, and he was the author of four books on Assyriology and a Hebrew word manual. Early in his years at Toronto Craig displayed a testiness toward university administrators. At the same time he seemed to see himself as the self-appointed adviser to President Falconer in matters relating to Taylor's department of Orientals, explaining to the president that he held his younger colleagues in low estimation because they had not been German-trained.

The trouble began in 1922, when Craig was retired after receiving two years' notice. Already displaying the animosity that subsequently made him an eccentric and pitiable recluse, he sued the university for fifty thousand dollars for arbitrary and unjust dismissal. His services, he protested, had been meritorious—he had missed only one lecture in five years—and further, the professorship conferred in 1916 gave him life tenure; he had been promised the chairmanship of the department; the board of governors should be replaced by democratic election; Falconer was incompetent, as were the teachers of the department.[1] Interviewed at his summer home by enthusiastic reporters from the Toronto press, Falconer denied that Craig had ever been promised the chairmanship and he defended the university's retirement policy.

From retirement and his cottage at Go-Home Bay in Muskoka, McCurdy intervened with a letter in the *Star* of 8 August defending the academic excellence of his former colleagues and accusing Craig of academic incompetence. When Falconer wrote to thank him, McCurdy replied with a nine-page typed letter, written over two days.[2] McCurdy, who had known and admired Craig in their Leipzig days, believed Craig was now "hopelessly paranoic" [sic]. The bulk of his letter, however, consisted of a remarkable statement of McCurdy's creed as a biblical scholar and teacher. The recent war had unsettled western civilization, and in the search for an explanation of events people virtually ignored the Bible. "Religious education was the primary motive and purpose in the creation of our Semitic department. . . . The intelligent study and teaching of the *essential* Bible should be a function of every university. . . . Unless Religion and science are first harmonized, they also will never be reconciled. . . . Such catholic use of the Bible" was the function of a Semitic department rather than theological schools.

McCurdy closed with a brief history of the department, emphasizing the losses suffered, from the death of McGee to the forced withdrawal of Benzinger, and strongly recommended that Craig's replacement be Arnot Stanley Orton, a scholar with the same high devotion, culture, achievements, and disposition as Taylor. Despite McCurdy's praise for Orton, who had studied at Harvard and in Jerusalem, served as a wartime chaplain, and returned to the working ministry, the position at University College went to another graduate, Theophile James Meek. After graduating from Toronto in 1903, Meek had spent three years at McCormick Theological Seminary and another two years in Germany—at Marburg, Leipzig, and finally Berlin, where he studied Assyriology. Returning to North America after a visit to Palestine, he taught in American institutions and received a Chicago Ph.D. for his thesis, "Old Babylonian Business and Legal Documents." In 1922 he

[1] *Telegram*, 25 July 1922; *Star*, 26 July 1922.
[2] UTA, Falconer Papers, Box 78, J. F. McCurdy to Sir R. A. Falconer, 4 September 1922.

had just been appointed head of Semitics at Bryn Mawr when the Craig episode occurred.

Meek had already been warmly recommended and seriously considered as a successor for Benzinger. Now he wrote from Chicago to Taylor in the summer of 1922 stating that be believed he could get out of the Byrn Mawr commitment to come to Toronto—"I have always remained a loyal Britisher despite my long residence abroad"—and that he hoped to return to Canada where he could pursue his interest in the growing field of the history of religions.[3] Meek's list of his teachers read like an international who's who of biblical studies—McCurdy, McFadyen, Friedrich Delitzsch, E. Sachau, Adolf Erman, Auguste Barth, Hermann Gunkel, Arthur Ungnad, Karl Budde, Eduard Lehmann-Haupt, Eduard Meyer, J. M. Smith, H. P. Smith, J. H. Breasted, D. D. Luckenbill, Julius A. Bewer, G. L. Robinson, and A. S. Carrier. His appointment, however, was complicated by the Craig case, which was finally settled in favor of the University of Toronto at the end of 1922. Meek took up his position with the rank of full professor at the start of the next academic year.

During the winter before the Craig case, Taylor had been seriously ill and his teaching duties were taken up by William Andrew Irwin, a graduate of Victoria College and Chicago, who was married to J. F. McLaughlin's daughter. In 1919 Irwin had been hired as a lecturer in the sensitive area of Oriental literature and history. Appreciative of the young man's support during his illness and of Irwin's popularity with the students, Taylor pressed for a promotion and permanent post for Irwin. One year later, in 1923, Irwin was promoted to assistant professor of Semitic languages, thus increasing the full-time staff of the department to three. Meek was teaching fourteen hours per week, Irwin eighteen, and Taylor twenty. A year later the University of Chicago offered Meek its chair of Hebrew language and literature, "convinced that he is the best man at present available in America."[4] Although Meek did not wish to leave Canada, Taylor used the occasion to ask for additional faculty, warning that Meek's departure would be an irreparable loss. "The science [of biblical studies]," he told the president, "has developed so rapidly and so widely within the last twenty-five years . . . much time must be given to investigation and interpretation of materials. Our University is one of the few of its size and importance where so little has been done in this respect." Two weeks later the board of governors raised Meek's salary another five hundred dollars.

Just two years later Taylor was offered the prestigious principalship of Queen's but declined because he felt the work of his department was so important not only for biblical studies as a discipline but also for "the

[3] Ibid., Box 80, T. J. Meek to W. R. Taylor, 21 July 1922; ibid., Box 45, G. E. Fellows to W. R. Taylor, 4 June 1915.

[4] Ibid., Box 85, W. R. Taylor to Sir R. A. Falconer, 9 April 1924.

Church as a whole," a reflection of his involvement (along with most Canadian biblical scholars) in the activities of the Student Christian Movement. No senior position was created, but through the use of teaching fellowships Taylor was able in the late twenties to promote the careers of promising young scholars, including Frederick Winnett and Stewart McCullough, both later prominent members of the department. In the same period the department made a concerted effort to hire Frank Wright Beare to teach Hellenistic Greek, a subject that had been added to the department's offerings a generation earlier and was taught by various members of the department although listed under classics. Beare, however, preferred to finish his theological training at Knox, after which he combined the working ministry and archeology before entering academic teaching in the thirties.

Taylor's unusual gifts as a teacher made his influence paramount in the formation of a new generation of biblical students at University College. He continued McCurdy's traditional emphasis on solid linguistic training as the foundation of scholarship. To one stumbling class in first-year Hebrew he exploded, "You don't get this by prayer and fasting but by hard work." More often he made his point with a humorous comment. "Imagination in archeology," he once remarked, "must operate according to well-defined principles. For example, the recently reported discovery at Jaffa of a pair of boots bearing the letter 'J' does not immediately establish the historicity of the tale of Jonah."[5] Like McCurdy and Falconer, Taylor approached biblical studies more philosophically than linguistically and his many articles—as often humanistic as technical—were polished gems of literary style. Like McCurdy before him, Taylor was so heavily burdened, even overworked, with teaching responsibilities that he never found sufficient time for research and publication. Although an inspiration to his students, he was occasionally accused of "upsetting students' ideas."[6] Quietly and with dedication the somewhat reserved Taylor followed McCurdy's footsteps in building up a department that in ability and comprehensiveness was unequaled in Canada at that time.

Outside of the classroom Taylor also perpetuated another of McCurdy's enthusiasms—amateur sport, an enthusiasm shared by most of that second generation of teachers of biblical studies in Toronto. For twenty-eight years McCurdy served as honorary president of student athletics at the university and reportedly never missed a football game (as late as his fiftieth year McCurdy played football with the Knox College students, and his knowledge of the history and personnel of intercollegiate football was "encyclopedic").[7] Taylor too was an enthusiastic follower of college football, while Meek, an ardent tennis player until the age of seventy-six, was the

[5] Private information from F. V. Winnett.

[6] R. B. Y. Scott, interviewed with W. S. McCullough and F. V. Winnett, 27 November 1979.

[7] *University of Toronto Monthly*, October 1935, p. 13.

outspoken opponent of professionalization in sports, especially at the university level (where he blamed the trend on American influences). At Victoria another contemporary, Sammy Hooke, was outstanding in several sports and once reportedly refused a chance to quadruple his salary by becoming a professional golfer.[8] J. F. McLaughlin of Victoria and his son-in-law, W. A. Irwin, were enthusiastic woodsmen and took extended canoe trips, sometimes accompanied by Hooke, who reveled in the Canadian outdoor life.

The same year that Meek arrived at University College, Trinity obtained a second appointment in the area of biblical studies. F. H. Cosgrave had taught Old and New Testament in both arts and divinity faculties since 1907 and since 1916 had also served as dean of divinity. His duties had been so heavy that in 1918 Trinity had enticed William Rollo, a prize winner in Hebrew, Arabic, and Syriac at Edinburgh and Glasgow, to come from the college of the Scottish Episcopal church where he had taught for twenty-seven years. Rollo was sixty-four when he moved to Trinity and now a decade later he was joined by Samuel Alfred Browne Mercer, who also accepted briefly Cosgrave's position as dean of divinity. A native of England but raised in Newfoundland, Mercer graduated in engineering from the University of Michigan but turned to theology and biblical studies, which he pursued at Wisconsin and Harvard.

Rollo seems to have published nothing—his only documented opinion, given when he applied for Benzinger's job, was that there was no future for him at Trinity—but Mercer was both productive and loquacious. By his retirement Mercer had written thirty-nine books and innumerable articles on biblical studies, had given uncounted public lectures (Cosgrave called him unequaled "in the art of popular exposition"),[9] and boasted that he had mastered perhaps fifty languages at the rate of two or three per year.[10] He did not associate, however, either professionally or socially with other biblical scholars in Canada. He was reputed to have married into money, and when his father-in-law supposedly threatened to excise Mercer from his will if he moved to Canada Mercer arranged to live and teach at Trinity at the college's expense for only two months of each term. He spent the rest of the year at a retreat in Grafton, Massachusetts, from where he later published the periodical *Aethiops* for a former student and wealthy patron, H. M. Hyatt. His Trinity students, however, alluding to Mercer's appreciation of whiskey, sang, "He came to Trinity because the U. S. A. was dry."[11]

Mercer was hired by Trinity because he was considered to be one of the world's leading Egyptologists. "His appointment," wrote Provost C. A. Seager,

[8] C. B. Sissons, *A History of Victoria University* (Toronto: University of Toronto Press, 1952) p. 263.

[9] *Trinity University Review* 59, no. 3 (Christmas 1946) 13.

[10] *Star Weekly*, 1 November 1930.

[11] *Trinity College Song Book*, 1937, p. 7.

"would mean a great contribution on Trinity's part to the intellectual life of the University of Toronto, which is weak along the lines in which Dr. Mercer is strong."[12] (The university did not have its own Egyptologist until after World War II.) Surprisingly, Mercer's appointment was opposed within the Church of England in Canada because of doubts about his orthodoxy. The bishop of Algoma relayed adverse comments to his fellow bishop of Ottawa, who warned Provost C. A. Seager of the rumors. "We ought to allow scope for Criticism of the O.T. so long as it is constructive and does not take the form of denials of Revelation and Inspiration," but any "uncertainty" regarding the creed, virgin birth, and resurrection would be "a clear disqualification for the office of training our students for the Ministry."[13] To the bishop of Toronto Mercer made both orally and in writing "an entirely satisfactory statement as to his position regarding the Faith of the Church"[14] and received forthwith his appointment as dean of theology and professor of Hebrew "and Egyptology." Exactly one year later Mercer resigned his deanship because he had discovered that administrative chores were death to research.[15]

Church Union and Biblical Studies

From 1902 to 1925 the Methodist, Presbyterian, and Congregational churches in Canada were engaged first in negotiations and then in legislative proceedings to create a unified Protestant and "national" church. Anglicans and Baptists had early decided not to join the church union movement, and almost from the outset it had been apparent that Presbyterian opinion was so sharply divided that schism might be the result if organic church union was achieved. The three denominations were approaching completion of the union when World War I began, and the union process did not get under way again until peace returned and until Presbyterian unionists decided nothing could be gained by further temporizing with their church's minority that was now so actively opposing union.

Complex property considerations in connection with church union required that enabling legislation be obtained from the Canadian parliament and from the legislature of each province, and by 1924 such legislation was placed before the politicians. The major battlefields for the dissidents were in Ontario and Quebec; elsewhere the proposals were passed into law without much trouble. The counteraction of the nonconcurring Presbyterians—about one-third of the church concentrated heavily in the urban areas of Quebec and throughout southern Ontario—achieved two victories in the Ontario legislature: provision was made for the legal continuance of a Presbyterian

[12] TCA, Seager Papers, file 21, C. A. Seager to L. W. B. Broughall, 28 May 1923.

[13] Ibid., J. C. Roper to C. A. Seager, 7 June 1923.

[14] Ibid., Report of the Special Committee to nominate a successor to Dean Cosgrave, 12 June 1923.

[15] Ibid., Sidney Jones Papers, S. A. B. Mercer to C. A. Seager, 2 May 1924.

church in Canada, and Knox College was secured to that church. This latter arrangement was a political trade-off in exchange for withdrawal of the strong antiunionist opposition to the property settlement that would have transferred all Presbyterian property to the new church. This concession regarding Knox College was later copied in 1926 by the Quebec legislature, which transferred Presbyterian College from the United Church back to the continuing Presbyterian church, thanks to antipathy toward Protestant church union on the part of Roman Catholic members of the legislature.

At Knox College every member of faculty and three-quarters of the student body joined the United Church when it was formed in June 1925, but continuing possession of the college buildings by the Presbyterians created several problems. Victoria's theological faculty had not been disturbed because the whole Methodist church entered union, while the former Knox faculty, including Richard Davidson, its Old Testament professor since 1910, was transformed into Union Theological College, federated to the University of Toronto. Davidson had proved himself a worthy pupil of McCurdy. More than half a century after church union he was remembered by his students as an inspired and inspiring teacher. For two years the old Knox faculty shared the college buildings with the continuing Presbyterians—a situation that may have created some tensions but no serious friction—but in 1927 Union Theological College moved across the campus to use Victoria's facilities. Two years later Union was merged with the theological faculty of Victoria University to form Emmanuel College.[16]

Through this merger the new college acquired a strong contingent of biblical scholars, almost an embarrassment of riches. McLaughlin and Davidson were already leading figures in the Old Testament field, as was Michael in New Testament. Knox was without a New Testament professor at the moment of union in 1925 since William Manson, the stimulating young teacher who had replaced Law, had returned to Scotland after only four years at the college. His place was now filled from the Presbyterian side by the appointment of John Dow, Scottish-born and a graduate of St. Andrews and of New College, Edinburgh. Dow had already published a New Testament study, *Jesus and the Human Conflict*, and arriving at Toronto he moved with the rest of the Knox faculty into the temporary Union Theological College and then into Emmanuel, where he had a distinguished career as teacher, author, and churchman.

For the continuing Presbyterian church it was necessary to rebuild the human resources of Knox after union, a process that required at least a generation because of staffing problems and the disaster of the depression. Thomas Eakin returned to teach Old Testament, but much of his usefulness and the harmony of the institution were lost between 1930 and 1936 as a

---

[16] K. H. Causland, *The Founding of Emmanuel College of Victoria University of the University of Toronto* (privately published, 1978) pp. 57–67.

result of his much publicized conflict with E. L. Morrow, the professor of church history. Eakin's retirement in 1944 and the retirement of John David Cunningham, professor of New Testament and Greek exegesis, opened a new era for Knox College. Cunningham had taught briefly in Knox, his alma mater, when William Caven died suddenly in 1904, and he had been runner-up to Robert Law for the New Testament chair in 1909. After church union he was called from the pastorate to join Eakin and two others as the reconstituted faculty of Knox College, but despite his earlier promise as a scholar, Cunningham seems to have made little impact on the academic community of biblical studies during the dismal years of the depression and World War II.

In Montreal a problem more serious than the Knox settlement arose within the cooperating colleges affiliated with McGill University. The last general assembly of the undivided Presbyterian church had fired the faculty of Presbyterian College at the beginning of June 1925 and had appointed an acting principal and a board of managers. Acting on a telegram from the assembly, Montreal unionists occupied the building and seized the college seal and records. Principal Daniel Fraser arrived home from Scotland hours later to find himself barred from his office by private police in the employ of the new board. The personal property of Fraser and Eakin was later restored to them, and with the support of the continuing Presbyterian church Fraser enlisted the help of faculty from McGill and Diocesan College to continue classes for the seven students who remained when the other five went into union. Eventually the Presbyterian College property was restored to the Presbyterian church, and Fraser commented that the temporary exile had brought the college into closer relations with McGill. In fact, however, Presbyterian College remained virtually isolated from its sister seminaries in Montreal because it withdrew from the joint board and did not enter again into cooperation until 1969.

The events at Presbyterian College seem to have increased the pressure to move from theological cooperation to a faculty of theology within McGill. The Anglicans now found themselves working not with three equal partners but with one large United Theological College formed from Wesleyan, Congregational, and Presbyterian colleges. Since Congregational College buildings were aging and the even older Presbyterian College complex had been secured to the continuing Presbyterians, the United Church needed a new building and the result was the opening of Divinity Hall in 1931. At the inaugural luncheon for the new building, both the guest, Sir Robert Falconer, and McGill's principal, Sir Arthur Currie, suggested that yet another step had been taken by the cooperating churches toward the formation of a university faculty of theology.[17]

[17] H. K. Markell, *The Faculty of Religious Studies, McGill University, 1948-1978* (Montreal: Faculty of Religious Studies, McGill University, 1979) p. 16.

Elsewhere in Canada the United Church absorbed the Presbyterian theological colleges without any serious problems. Where surplus faculty resulted from the union of the three churches all professors were normally retained and numbers allowed to decline naturally by death and retirement. Manitoba College was merged with Wesley College to form the new United College at Winnipeg. Westminster Hall in Vancouver was renamed Union College, but the other former Presbyterian colleges—Pine Hill in Halifax, Queen's, St. Andrew's in Saskatoon—continued to function under their previous names. After Robertson College (Presbyterian) and Alberta College South (Methodist theological) had temporarily merged as United Theological College of Alberta, the new union institution for theological education in Alberta, renamed St. Stephen's, was affiliated to the provincial university in 1927. In addition to Victoria and Wesley, the Methodists brought into the union Mount Allison at Sackville, so that the new church in its early years could boast of three universities (two with theological faculties) and eight theological colleges.

The fact that among Presbyterians a higher precentage of clergy than of laity entered the United Church in 1925 was a significant feature of the union. Most of those who would be classed as supporters of higher criticism, both professors and working clergy, left the Presbyterian church and along with liberal Methodists and Congregationalists created in the new denomination a climate highly sympathetic to critical biblical studies and to the propagation of a parallel receptive attitude among the United Church laity. Popularly, and partly unjustly, the continuing Presbyterian church acquired and to a degree rejoiced in its reputation as being conservative biblically and theologically. Church union enriched biblical studies in Canada because it brought together the differing approaches and traditions of biblical interpretation from the three denominations and offered younger scholars the broadening experience of a more varied religious heritage. "One of the richest rewards of union," commented Davidson, "has been the opportunity to share in the life and friendship of J. F. McLaughlin."[18] At University College, however, the faculty in Orientals found less and less contact with biblical scholars in the affiliated theological colleges, not because of church union so much as the simple fact of physical growth in the university federation. The one important means of contact between the two groups was created soon after church union when the Canadian Society of Biblical Studies was founded in 1932.

Some Controversial Scholars

At Toronto a few of the biblical scholars projected very controversial images in the twenties. Victoria College's Sammy Hooke was the talk of

[18] Quoted in Causland, *Founding of Emmanuel College*, p. 96.

students and staff alike. An athlete of great achievements, he annually challenged all comers at the college to beat him on the tennis courts. Perhaps the most disconcerting facet of his muscular activities was his habit of retiring to the Little Vic ice rink at every opportunity, whereupon a note on his classroom door would inform knowledge-hungry students that education was suspended because "Professor Hooke has gone skating." Hooke believed in publicizing his discipline outside the ivy-cluttered walls—at the 1923 Toronto Skating Club Carnival he appeared in costume as King Tut, accompanied by an attractive "Queen Seti." Hooke was also reputed to be one of the best chess players in Toronto and a poet of great potential if only he would apply himself seriously. He had become a family friend of his senior colleague, J. F. McLaughlin, and of McLaughlin's son-in-law, W. A. Irwin, and frequently accompanied them on extended canoe trips through the Muskoka lakes.

W. R. Matthews, writing an "Appreciation" for Hooke's Festschrift, believed that those Canadian years so filled with outdoor activities were formative for Hooke, a time "of great happiness and widening mental horizons. . . . He found satisfaction in the work and evidently left a mark upon the University."[19] Hooke's mark was based on more than his athletic prowess and cultural accomplishments. "He was . . . gnomish in features as at times in behaviour," wrote C. B. Sissons even during Hooke's lifetime.[20] No doubt Hooke was a gadfly in classes, where he lectured despite a speech impediment to impressionable youths, and also in the Student Christian Movement, which he and most of his fellow biblical scholars at Toronto supported. He attended and spoke at SCM meetings (with W. Harold Reid and Gertrude Rutherford he took part in the 1921 national conference), was a contributor to that sounding board for the theology of social activism, *The Canadian Forum*, and was a founder of the student-faculty paper significantly named *The Rebel*, which flourished from 1917 to 1920 on the Toronto campus. Hooke may have represented a radical minority position in the SCM, but he gave the movement's meetings "a surprising twist" by his "puckish interventions" and by proposals such as turning a prayer room into a swear room.[21]

In the end, it was "the extreme radicalism of his views of scriptural exegesis"[22] that caused Hooke's removal, amid rumors and speculations, from the discreetly liberal atmosphere of Victoria College. In 1924 Hooke received a Rockefeller fellowship, with a promise of fifteen hundred dollars

[19] F. F. Bruce, ed., *Promise and Fulfillment* (Edinburgh: T. & T. Clark, 1963) p. 2.

[20] Sissons, *History of Victoria University*, p. 263.

[21] Ibid.; Bruce, *Promise and Fulfillment*, pp. 2–3; Richard Allen, *The Social Passion: Religion and Social Reform in Canada 1914–28* (Toronto: University of Toronto Press, 1971) pp. 222, 302–4, 310; Margaret Beattie, *A Brief History of the Student Christian Movement in Canada* (n.p., 1975) p. 78.

[22] *Star*, 15 January 1927.

from Victoria on the apparent understanding that he would not return to Toronto. Three years later he informed the board of regents that his anticipated job had not materialized and he wanted extra teaching to cover money lost during his leave. Instead the board sent him fifteen hundred dollars and washed its hands.[23] No public notice was taken of Hooke's departure (even his resignation is unrecorded) and so the public image of Victoria remained unsullied and undisturbed.

The university had been spared any mischievous attention from the Toronto press at the time of Sammy Hooke's departure thanks to the discretion exercised by Victoria's board of regents. In the spring of 1928, however, the newspapers delightedly reported that William Irwin, the *enfant terrible* of Orientals at University College, had read a paper to the American Oriental Society meeting in Washington, entitled "Truth in Ancient Israel," in which he accused certain Old Testament authors of having lied in the inspired scriptures. Always quick to test the public pulse, *Star* reporters solicited opinions on Irwin's paper from local clergymen.[24] The popular evangelist, E. Crossley Hunter, regretted Irwin's language very much. The Reverend Stuart Parker of St. Andrew's Presbyterian Church was more outspoken. "[Irwin] attempts to judge the past by his own modern standards," he complained. "Why it's like cutting your grandfather's throat because he is old and doddering. . . . His attitude," concluded Parker, "to me sounds like a school boy's attempt to be terribly naughty." Rabbi Isserman of Holy Blossom Synagogue added noncommittally, "I hope Professor Irwin does not get into any trouble because of his statement. He is too good a man." When letters to the editor of the *Star* accused Irwin of blasphemy, Irwin finally retorted that the press account of his scholarly paper had been "misleading." [25]

Almost immediately Irwin compounded his own difficulties with his examination for second-year students. "To what extent may the stories of Noah, of Abraham and of Moses be accepted as dependable history?" asked one question. Another read, "Is the book of Jonah history, allegory or what is it? What do you think of the incident of the 'big fish'?" Chairman Taylor informed President Falconer that the examination with its "unfortunate" questions had fallen into the hands of the Toronto *Star*. With restrained annoyance the president replied, "It is unfortunate that in a subject that has to be handled with such care he did not show more discretion." Falconer could be sure that the *Star* would show no more discretion than Irwin had.[26]

Throughout Irwin's troubles the university authorities had been publicly

[23] Victoria College, Bursar's Office, Minutes of the Board of Regents, 1911–28, p. 261, 28 September 1925; ibid., pp. 328–30, 6 September 1927.

[24] *Star*, 17, 24 April 1928.

[25] Ibid., 3 May 1928.

[26] UTA, Falconer Papers, Box 110, W. R. Taylor to Sir R. A. Falconer, 15 May 1928; ibid., Sir R. A. Falconer to W. R. Taylor, 29 May 1928.

silent but undoubtedly embarrassed at the popular reaction to the professor's activities. Just one year later the board of governors was placed in an even more awkward position by another of its esteemed biblical scholars, but not because of his higher criticism. A public rally of communists had been announced for the evening of 27 August 1929 in Queen's Park, and the civic authorities had banned the meeting, warning all law-abiding citizens to avoid the area. Nevertheless, about 8:00 P.M. Professor Theophile J. Meek left his home, crossed the university campus, and about a half hour later was caught up in a large crowd of alleged demonstrators being herded westward along College Street by some of Toronto's finest.[27] Apparently the rally had not really gone beyond singing the Internationale and a few similar proletarian anthems before the mayor and a hastily assembled body of police began to move the crowds away. One boy was slapped by a constable for singing "We'll hang [Police] Chief Draper to a sour apple tree" and other parodies with less polite lyrics. As another constable ordered the mass of humanity to move faster, Professor Meek retorted that that was a physical impossibility. For this he was supposedly rewarded with a shove and an oath. "None of your g—d— lip," added the constable, but when Meek tried to write that in his notebook along with a transcript of the constable's undeleted expletives, the officer apparently seized Meek's wrists and tried to grab his notes.

This incident was reported by two observant *Star* journalists, but Chief Draper announced hours later that he had received no complaint from Meek. At the local police station the constable was not available for comment. The next day Meek and Draper did meet face to face, but after being interviewed by the chief the professor stated bluntly, "We did not get anywhere."[28] His complaint was then formally lodged, and in October the Toronto police commissioners opened a probe that heard seventeen witnesses on Meek's behalf at two different sittings. After due deliberation the commissioners announced in November that the allegations had been dismissed on the grounds that the evidence presented by Meek, two reporters, and the battery of witnesses was inconclusive. The professor told the press he was "absolutely unsatisfied," and wrote to the provincial attorney general demanding a parliamentary investigation. This request was refused.[29]

The university had not interfered in the Meek affair, and there is no written record of the feelings of the august board of governors nor of the ever-proper president, Sir Robert Falconer. But the memory and perhaps the odor of the episode lingered on and just two months later public opinion, the press, the university administration, and another member of the Orientals department were in the limelight. On 10 January 1930 Bill Irwin announced his departure from Toronto for the University of Chicago and

[27] *Star*, 28 August 1929.
[28] Ibid., 30 August 1929.
[29] *Telegram*, 4 October 1929; *Star*, 8 November 1929; *Mail*, 16 November 1929.

"greater opportunity." In an interview with *The Varsity* five days later Irwin explained that a university exists to promote inquiry but that the University of Toronto as an institution refused to protect that freedom. In Irwin's opinion the university was "obsessed with a ruinous caution" and "is mildewed with discretion." He cited as examples of this failure to protect scholars the recent Meek affair and his own persecution for another "utterly innocuous" paper that he had delivered at a departmental meeting. Press reports of his paper had occasioned condemnatory letters to the university and even to the minister of education. "*Mirabile dictu*," said Irwin, why the minister of education? Irwin had been called in for consultation then, and although his statement of the incident was accepted as "entirely satisfactory," he had been warned that any public comment he might make would not be supported by the university.

The *Varsity* immediately demanded an investigation of "the seeming political control" of the university. As always the *Star* sought out all opinions fit to print but discovered that the university officials refused to reply to either Irwin or *The Varsity*.[30] Not discouraged, the *Star* reporters moved at once to the nearby provincial legislative building in search of comment, only to be told by Premier George Howard Ferguson that it was solely a matter for the university or its president. When informed of what Irwin had said concerning the bacteriological rot infesting the university, Ferguson commented, "Well, if he holds those views, perhaps it is just as well that he is leaving. I don't think I know him." When reminded of the previous controversy over Irwin's Old Testament interpretations, Ferguson's memory returned. "Oh yes. . . . Well, the University will just have to get along without him."

The busy reporters hastened back to the university campus and managed to corner the president. "I have nothing to say whatever," was Falconer's reply. His heir apparent, H. J. Cody, then chairman of the board, referred all inquiries to the principal of University College, but Principal Maurice Hutton contented himself with the announcement that Irwin's statement was "rather absurd." The unanimous declaration of members of the board was "no comment," although one did explain, "It is well known that public opinion is influenced or intimidated by university opinions." Only one voice was raised in Irwin's defense: A. T. De Lury, mathematician and dean of arts, insisted that it was the board's reponsibility to defend its faculty, including Meek and Irwin. Everyone, De Lury believed, was in Irwin's debt because he had had the courage to speak out. The same day that it printed its rash of interviews, the *Star* also published a cartoon depicting Irwin as a naughty boy who had just knocked a mortar board from the head of Premier Ferguson with a snowball. The mortar board was labeled "Varsity" and carried a placard reading, "A POLITICAL BOSSISM."

[30] *Star*, 16 January 1930.

The last word, however, came from Montreal, where an editorial in the *Standard* described Irwin as an "ambitious young radical" (he was forty-six) seeking publicity through martyrdom. The *Standard* was sure that twenty years later Irwin would thank the University of Toronto for "being mildewed with descretion" and for taking no notice of "his immature opinions."[31] Thus ended the Irwin incident. The voice of the people had been heard more loudly than the whisper from the ivory tower. Discretion still outweighed valor in university circles, but in any case the depression had arrived and jobs were hard to find, especially for higher critics.

The Founding of the CSBS

One product of the postwar interest in religion and of the sense of Canadian nationalism that developed during the war was the founding of a distinctive Canadian quarterly periodical to serve the academic interests of biblical studies, theology, church history, and other religion-centered disciplines. The *Canadian Journal of Religious Thought*—its title accurately reflected the liberal theological climate of the generation—began publication in 1924 with George B. King as editor and Richard Davidson as business manager, and a board drawn from five Protestant denominations. In its first volume 20 percent of the articles came from biblical scholars and in succeeding years this proportion did not vary much. The Toronto scholars were heavily represented but Queen's, McMaster, and McGill were also there. Only two biblical scholars from outside Canada were included— Canadian-born Shirley Jackson Case and William Manson. Not all these articles were on biblical topics. Falconer, for instance, contributed a revealing item about his student days in Germany with his brother and H. A. A. Kennedy.

The *Journal* survived the first shock of the Great Depression, but by 1932 its financial state had become critical. In an editorial entitled "The End of an Episode" the managers announced that declining subscriptions made it impossible to publish the periodical any longer unless some wealthy patron were found. None was, but meanwhile other approaches to the problem of academic isolation were being explored as the editors of the *Journal* had promised. One of those approaches was the idea of forming a national association of biblical scholars. Given the shortage of funds for travel there was little hope that scholars outside of central Canada would be able to attend any meetings of such a society, but correspondence would be better than no contact whatsoever within the academic community.

The impetus to form such an association came largely from the faculty of the University of Toronto and its affiliated theological colleges. When nine individuals, "the founding fathers," met at Emmanuel College on

---

[31] *Standard*, 25 January 1930.

3 March 1933 to take positive steps in the direction of a biblical studies society, University College's Department of Semitics was represented by T. J. Meek and his junior colleagues W. S. McCullough and Frederick Winnett; Emmanuel College by Principal Davidson, J. H. Michael, and John Dow; Wycliffe by Charles V. Pilcher; Trinity by John Lowe; and R. B. Y. Scott had come from United Theological College in Montreal. Four of this group—Meek, Michael, Lowe, and Scott—were appointed an executive committee to draft a constitution and arrange an organizational meeting. By 15 April Scott as secretary was able to mail an invitation to interested persons to meet at Victoria College to create a Canadian society of biblical studies and to join in symposia on "The Problem of the Exile" and "The Lucan Documents." Dinner would be available for "about seventy-five cents."[32] Writing of the event thirty-three years later, R. B. Y. Scott recalled:

> When the Society was organized in 1933, the then senior Biblical scholars in Canada readily responded to the suggestion that a society be formed to encourage Canadian Biblical scholarship, and they generously supported the younger group whose idea this was. We felt that too few were able to enjoy the stimulus of the meetings in the United States of the long-established Society of Biblical Literature and Exegesis, and that Canadian scholarship would be encouraged if there were in existence also an organization of our own. The long-term results have certainly justified this hope.[53]

The inaugural meeting of the society was held in the Senior Common Room of Victoria's Burwash Hall on 2 and 3 May with Sir Robert Falconer in the chair. An amended constitution was adopted by twenty-one of the twenty-three charter members on the first evening, when Falconer was elected president, Scott was chosen secretary-treasurer, G. Abbot-Smith vice-president, and W. R. Taylor and J. H. Michael were added to the roster as "Other Executive." The following morning four papers on the exile were read and four on the Lucan documents that afternoon. The Canadian Society of Biblical Studies was now an established fact of Canadian scholarly interests.

Within the next two months membership in the society was doubled by the addition of twenty-four more members, most of them from outside Toronto and including E. F. Scott and William Irwin, who resided in New York and Chicago respectively. Of the forty-six charter members enrolled by the Canadian Society of Biblical Studies seventeen were primarily connected with universities; another fourteen were affiliated with seminaries, eight including four rabbis (Julius Berger, Harry Stern, and H. Abramowitz from Montreal, and Maurice Eisendrath of Toronto) could be classed as "working clergy"; and the remaining eight held various positions, including church- and university-related posts. The only woman, Gertrude Rutherford,

---

[32] CSBS Records, file, John Macpherson, "A History of the Canadian Society of Biblical Studies," presidential address to the CSBS, 1962; rev. version published in *The Bulletin*, 1967, pp. 1–16.

[33] R. B. Y. Scott, *The Bulletin*, 1967, p. iv.

was in this last group, and she and T. J. Meek appear to have made the lone twosome from the laity. Nineteen members listed themselves as doctors of divinity (Falconer preferred his more exclusive title of Knight Commander of St. Michael and St. George), others noted their Ph.D.'s or Th.D.'s or simply called themselves "Doctor." The ones who signed neither "Reverend" nor "Doctor" were Miss Rutherford and one very modest "Mister," W. S. McCullough, M.A.

As might be expected in the new society, not only were the majority of members in the academic professions but most—twenty-six in fact—came from Toronto, with six more from Montreal and four from Hamilton. Only seven were from the West (three each from Winnipeg and Vancouver, and one from Saskatoon), while W. G. Watson of Pine Hill Divinity Hall was the sole representative from the Maritime provinces. The one charter member with the longest association in biblical studies in Canada—a substantial shadow from a bygone age—was G. C. Workman, in his eighty-fifth year with three more years of life ahead of him. Of the original forty-six members of the society over half came from the United Church—not surprisingly in view of the ecumenical theology that informed that denomination. In addition to the four rabbis drawn from contemporary liberal Judaism, the Anglican and Baptist communions were well represented, but significantly absent was any member of the continuing Presbyterian church.

"In the face of mass bankruptcy in business, and in spite of all the discouragements of the Depression," President John MacPherson wrote at the society's thirtieth birthday,

> these enthusiasts confidently organized the Canadian Society of Biblical Studies. Why were these scholars so presumptuous? One stimulus was doubtless economic in origin. There were at that time very few agencies with funds to assist members of the academic community to attend meetings of learned societies; and limited salaries prevented at least the younger scholars from travelling to professional associations abroad. Only eleven of the charter members belonged to the Society of Biblical Literature and Exegesis of New York. A partial explanation was to be found in the youthful enthusiasm of some of the pioneers; for although most of the older members of 1933 had been trained abroad, several of their younger colleagues were representatives of the first generation of Canadian-trained Biblical scholars. Another stimulus doubtless derived from the pioneer nature of the project itself. This was the first Canadian interconfessional scholarly society concerned with the religious sciences, deliberately aiming from the outset to be national in scope. Though it was a theological society which had been first envisaged, it was (perhaps providentially) a Biblical society which first emerged. Barth's *Kirchliche Dogmatik* had not then appeared in English . . . , nor had the "Divino Afflante Spiritu" yet been promulgated . . . ; and the new Canadian society helped to direct attention to the Biblical basis of theology several years before these two powerful stimuli began to exert their extensive influence.[34]

The youthful enthusiasm of the young society and its executive was reflected in a letter dated 23 June (just six weeks after the inaugural

[34] *The Bulletin*, 1967, pp. 2–3.

meeting) calling for papers for the second annual meeting, to be held at Toronto in May 1934. Twenty-one members came to this second meeting, where seventeen papers were read, including four from absentee authors as far afield as Edmonton and New Brunswick. The financial constraints of the day were, however, very evident; all but four of the participants were from Toronto, the exceptions being George King of Winnipeg, Chancellor H. P. Whidden and H. L. MacNeill from McMaster in Hamilton, and the society's energetic secretary-treasurer from Montreal.

Perhaps of necessity the thematic approach to programming was not repeated in 1934 nor at the third annual meeting, held like its predecessors at Burwash Hall. In 1935, however, the society began publication of an annual *Bulletin*. The first number of the *Bulletin* had twenty-one printed pages and contained two papers, by Falconer and Maurice N. Eisendrath. The following year's issue carried three papers and a membership list, while the third number, in 1937, included a program from the recent annual meeting. This pattern continued until the outbreak of the war when publication was suspended for a year for lack of funds, thus robbing the would-be historian of George B. King's paper on Canadian crises in higher criticism. When Number Six was issued in December 1941, it had only eight mimeographed pages with minutes and synopses of papers from the 1940 and 1941 meetings. The printing of papers (now four in number) was resumed in 1943 and two years later a list of members was again included, but the practice was not repeated for another fifteen years. Although the papers printed in the *Bulletin* and the others presented at the annual meetings of the CSBS were predominantly on Old Testament topics, New Testament subjects were included, and part of the 1944 session was devoted to pedagogical problems connected with teaching biblical studies in colleges and schools other than theological seminaries.

Before the society's second meeting, in 1934 the executive had decided to levy a one-dollar registration fee to be used "to pay a proportion of travelling expenses of members attending from outside the place of meeting," to a maximum of ten dollars per member.[35] Although the society's membership rose steadily until by 1940 it had almost one hundred on the roll (a third of whom were in arrears with dues), attendance at the annual meetings in Toronto averaged between twenty and twenty-five. A purging of the roll in 1941 reduced the membership to seventy-four (of whom only forty-five had paid the current year's fee). The treasurer normally collected about one hundred dollars annually from all sources but spent three-quarters of this to print the *Bulletin* until the mimeographed format was adopted during the early war years.

"The significance of this program of publication," MacPherson noted with reference to the *Bulletin*, "must be measured by the contemporary

scarcity of comparable publications. At the time those interested in following the development of biblical scholarship in Canada had nothing to read
except denominational and college announcements. Only a very few
Canadian scholars had published in the available American professional
journals."[36] The problem of lack of outlets for Canadian scholarly work was
not new in the 1930s—it had been one motive for the creation of the Society
of Biblical Studies—and if the situation has improved since World War II
the problem has certainly not disappeared. Nevertheless Canadians were
able to publish in several journals during the depression and the war.

Reminiscing about the early years of the Canadian Society of Biblical
Studies R. B. Y. Scott (who served as secretary-treasurer for seven years)
commented, "Although it was often like pulling their teeth to get papers out
of potential contributors, the meetings were always worth the trouble."[37]
Even if the thematic programming was not stressed by the society at its
meetings, those gatherings still possessed a cohesive element in the lively
Canadian interest in contemporary scholarly biblical issues. The publication
in English of Martin Dibelius's work on form criticism and the appearance
of C. C. Torrey's *The Four Gospels* (1933) prompted two of the papers at
the fourth meeting in 1936. Form criticism continued to be a subject for
discussion for a decade, and at the same time new textual materials were
noted and examined by members. Frank Beare gave five papers in the space
of seven years on the Chester Beatty manuscripts.

On the eve of World War II a Canadian branch of the Society of Biblical Literature was formed in connection with the CSBS after thirty-three
members expressed an interest in such a step and the parent society in the
United States had given its approval.[38] In fact, in 1939 all but ten members
of the new group were previously members of the SBL in the United
States. Not all members of the CSBS joined the SBL Canadian Section, and
over the years the section had an increasing proportion of members who
did not belong to the CSBS. Despite this discrepancy the executives of the
two groups were always identical after 1941 thanks to a resolution to that
effect adopted at the section's second meeting. No significant changes in the
structure of the CSBS were made as a result of the establishment of the
SBL Canadian Section, but in its own programs the CSBS reflected a
broadening of interests in its choice of presidents and in the subjects of the
presidential addresses. Rabbi Maurice N. Eisendrath, elected president in
May 1939, gave his address the following year on "The Biblical Basis of
Democracy's Present Struggle." These developments both in publishing and
programming may seem relatively unimportant, but they were harbingers
of the postwar expansion of biblical studies that emphasized areas of

[36] *The Bulletin*, 1967, pp. 3–4.
[37] Ibid., p. iv.
[38] CSBS Records, file 3, Executive Minutes, 1937ff.

research formerly secondary to the traditional predominance of Old Testament interests.

Canadian Scholars at Home and Abroad

At the end of World War I, F. H. Wallace predicted that Canadians would no longer wish to pursue biblical studies in Germany,[39] but before the close of the twenties several Canadian graduate students in biblical studies did take up that traditional scholarly connection, including W. Harold Reid, who spent 1929–30 at Tübingen and Strasbourg, and James D. Smart, who was in Marburg for the same academic year along with Samuel MacLean Gilmour. For many Canadians work in the biblical field was capped by a Ph.D. from the University of Toronto, but a number of young scholars of this generation were attracted to Chicago for further study.

The University of Chicago's reputation had been built over the period of that watershed generation by the distinctive contributions of William Rainey Harper, James Henry Breasted, John D. Rockefeller, Shailer Mathews, and Shirley Jackson Case. As a Hebrew scholar and president of the university from 1891 to 1906, Harper had pushed the development of biblical studies much as McCurdy and Falconer had done at Toronto. Breasted, professor of Oriental languages and assistant director of the university's Haskell Oriental Museum after 1901, had promoted a comprehensive or integrated plan for Near Eastern studies. Rockefeller by his generous bequests to the university after 1892 had provided the lubrication for the academic machinery and especially for postgraduate research and archeological exploration through his funding of the Oriental Institute. It was Mathews and Case, however, who had substantially reshaped the course of biblical studies—Mathews by his easy assumption of a harmony between biblical radicalism and blatant evangelicalism, and Case by his pursuit of "a distinctive methodology and a grand overview of history."[40]

Despite the attraction of biblical studies at Chicago there was still such a marked conservatism in the Canadian approach to the discipline that contemporary students seemed satisfied to have had their first encounter with higher criticism within the walls of Canadian institutions. "Certainly [Chicago's influence]," wrote H. P. Whidden, a product of its graduate school and a future chancellor of McMaster University, "is not what we, who have the ideals that McMaster cherishes, believe should be exerted. . . . It is not exactly a hot-bed of Heresy, and yet pretty tall heretics have grown there and will continue to grow there for some time. For a man who has thought through . . . things a little, it is not a very dangerous place; but I am

[39] *Star*, 25 March 1920.

[40] R. W. Funk, "The Watershed of the American Biblical Tradition The Chicago School, First Phase, 1892–1920," *Journal of Biblical Literature* 95 (1976) 14, 15.

quite satisfied that I did not take my regular Theological Course there."[41] In a large measure one product of this Chicago connection was the recrudescence of the "modernist" controversy that had troubled McMaster in the first decade of the century. The pressure on McMaster University because of the alleged modernism of I. G. Matthews, J. H. Farmer, and other professors had abated during the war years because of the national preoccupation with the war effort and perhaps also because of the death of Elmore Harris, the most effective of the Canadian conservatives. With the return of peace came also an occasion to reopen the issue of modernism among Canadian Baptists. T. T. Shields, pastor of the wealthy Jarvis Street Church in Toronto, a spellbinding preacher and heir to Harris's mantle among his own denomination, seized the opportunity to take the reins of leadership among conservative Baptists when it became known in 1921 that Howard P. Whidden, president of Brandon College, was being considered for the chancellorship of McMaster.

Whidden, a Chicago graduate, "evangelical" liberal and an accepted theologian of the social gospel, was already involved in an investigation of the orthodoxy of Brandon College and of the teaching of Harris Lachlan MacNeill, its professor of New Testament interpretation, who had earlier taken leave from the college in order to do doctoral studies at Chicago. T. T. Shields supported the western critics of Brandon College, because to him the issue could not be localized. Thus, when Whidden's name was placed before the board of McMaster and the Baptist Convention, Shields was ready to launch an attack on "modernism," "liberalism," and "heresy" at McMaster. Whidden refused to lock horns directly with a man who, he had been warned, "has no scruples about twisting things to suit his own purposes."[42] Shields and his congregation (already depleted by its pastor's theology and maneuvering) withheld financial support from the university when Whidden was confirmed in the chancellorship.

The conferring of an honorary degree on W. H. P. Faunce, president of Brown University, at Whidden's installation was the next occasion for controversy. Shields denounced Faunce as a modernist and blamed Whidden and Farmer for this insult to Baptist orthodoxy. As Shields's campaign gathered vehemence and nationwide support, Whidden and McMaster found the resolve of the Baptist Convention faltering in 1924. I. G. Matthews, now at Crozer Seminary, still believed Shields had "about run [his] course,"[43] but the appointment to McMaster of L. H. Marshall, a liberal theologian with extensive training at Marburg and Berlin, gave Shields a further opportunity in 1925, coincident with the Scopes "monkey trial," to

---

[41] Quoted in C. M. Johnston, *McMaster University Volume 1/The Toronto Years* (Toronto: University of Toronto Press, 1976) pp. 93–94.

[42] Quoted, ibid., p. 173.

[43] Ibid., p. 180.

continue his attacks on the university. Again Shields was defeated but the split in Baptist ranks had deepened. The victory for McMaster may have cleared the theological air in the university, but it was paid for dearly in the widespread loss of denominational support. Four years later, as another campaign was being planned (along the lines of the older Matthews incident) to impugn Marshall's spirituality, the cause of the controversy resigned for lack of public confidence and returned to England.[44]

Although biblical studies had been only indirectly involved in the attacks on Brandon and McMaster by Shields and his fundamentalist supporters, the subsequent translation in 1933 of H. L. MacNeill, another McMaster-Chicago graduate, from Brandon to McMaster to teach New Testament confirmed the latter institution's position among other Canadian universities that were open to biblical studies through "frank, scientific discussion." The rise of interest in "Barthianism" or neo-orthodoxy among Canadian theologians during the 1930s and later did not have any direct influence on the development of biblical studies in Canadian universities. For a number of years in fact no "Barthians" were to be found on the faculties of Canadian theological colleges except W. W. Bryden at Knox, and this was the case at least until after 1945.[45] As for those scholars working in departments of Orientals or Near Eastern studies such as that in the University of Toronto, their approach to the Bible was of a markedly different character from that of their theological colleagues. The historical sense of continuum and causal relations, implicit in the older expression "historical criticism," provided philosophic approaches for the biblical scholars that were different from the kind of "timelessness" espoused by many if not most biblical theologians. This fundamental dichotomy, however, was not clearly apparent until after World War II when a rapprochement of the two points of view was attempted with good will but little success.

During the interwar years two new journals in the field of biblical studies were established—the *Journal of Bible and Religion* (1937) and the *Catholic Biblical Quarterly* (1938)—but aside from contributing articles to the CSBS *Bulletin* Canadian scholars seem to have confined their publications before 1945 to the *Journal of Biblical Literature*, the *American Journal of Semitic Languages* (of which T. J. Meek was associate editor throughout the 1930s), and the *Bulletin of the American Schools of Oriental Research*. The first of these carried articles by Meek, Falconer, R. B. Y. Scott, James D. Smart and F. W. Beare the second carried two major articles by W. E. Staples, and the *Bulletin* of the A.S.O.R contained two by Meek during the war years. While the number of periodical articles by Canadians increased after World War I, Canadians seem to have published fewer major works. Undoubtedly the most important Canadian

---

[44] Ibid.

[45] R. B. Y. Scott, interviewed with W. S. McCullough and F. V. Winnett, 27 November 1979.

monograph of the period was Meek's *Hebrew Origins* (1936), but a decade earlier W. G. Jordan of Queen's had published *History and Revelation*, and in 1921 G. Abbott-Smith had issued the first of many editions of his *Manual Greek Lexicon of the New Testament*, "a monumental work of rich scholarship" whose publication "gave its author an international reputation."[46] Meek was one of the four scholars chosen by the University of Chicago Press to prepare *The Bible: An American Translation*, which appeared in 1927. Many years later Meek undertook a complete revision of the *Translation* but regrettably circumstances prevented the publication of his work. The most significant joint cooperative publication was the *Abingdon Bible Commentary* (1929), which contained seven articles by Canadians—John Dow, A. R. Gordon, W. G. Jordan, and J. F. McLaughlin—and articles by three other scholars with Canadian connections—J. E. McFadyen, G. L. Robinson, and E. F. Scott (who had left Queen's for Union Theological Seminary, New York, in 1919). T. J. Meek was the only Canadian to contribute to the *New Schaff-Hertzog*.

Canadian scholars were frequent attenders and occasional contributors to meetings of the American Oriental Society and the Society of Biblical Literature and Exegesis. Since travel grants were scarce, the cost of such trips was often paid by the individual—Meek spent $34.50 in 1926 to attend a session in Philadelphia! On at least one occasion the Canadians were hosts to their American colleagues. The American Oriental Society gathered at Toronto in 1930 after two years of planning for a meeting described as "one of the most successful and pleasant" in the history of the society.[47]

By the time of the depression, Canadian biblical scholars were also gaining recognition internationally in the growing field of biblical archeology. W. R. Taylor, following in McCurdy's footsteps, was appointed annual professor at the American School of Oriental Research in Jerusalem for 1929–30. T. J. Meek spent the following year in the same office with the American School at Baghdad. He served as epigrapher to the expedition to Nuzi and later published the oldest map that had been discovered there. Materials from this dig were brought back for the Royal Ontario Museum and also for classroom use. En route home in 1932 Meek attended an international congress of Orientalists at Leiden as representative of the University of Toronto. A year later he gave two papers on his Iraq expedition at the American Oriental Society meeting and in 1935 published a volume of texts from Nuzi.[48] Meek was later involved in excavations planned for Tepe Gawra in Iraq, but these were cancelled at the outbreak of World War II. In

[46] Oswald Howard, *Montreal Diocesan Theological College: A History from 1873* (Montreal: McGill University Press, 1963) p. 122.
[47] UTA, Falconer Papers, Box 120, W. A. Irwin to Sir R. A. Falconer, 8 May 1930.
[48] Ibid., Box 127, T. J. Meek to Sir R. A. Falconer, 16 December 1930, 4 May 1931; ibid., Box 132, Meek to Falconer, 9 November 1931, 4 April 1932.

1931 F. W. Beare did archeological work in Egypt, and W. A. Potter of Victoria College visited Egypt and Palestine that year during a leave of absence but died in Edinburgh on his way home.

In 1938 Fred Winnett was made an honorary fellow of the Jerusalem School of Oriental Research, and two other Toronto graduates won Thayer fellowships to the American Schools as well during the interwar years. William Ewart Staples, a former Victoria student who returned from war service to enter graduate work, won a fellowship in 1921–22, an honor which Taylor called "a remarkable achievement."[49] Staples returned to teach in secondary schools for several years, but in 1928 he joined the Megiddo expedition of the Oriental Institute of the University of Chicago. On the retirement of J. F. McLaughlin, Staples was appointed to Victoria College (McLaughlin was the last appointee to hold the double position in arts and theology after Emmanuel College replaced Victoria's theological faculty). The other Thayer fellowship was won by Kenneth Charles Evans in 1932 on completion of his Ph.D. at Toronto Evans subsequently taught at Trinity College and served there as dean of divinity; he also was president of the CSBS and in 1952 was elected bishop of Ontario.

It was S. A. B. Mercer, the only Canadian present at the opening of Tutankhamen's tomb,[50] who reported the most spectacular single-handed research achievement of any Canadian. Mercer wanted to publish a critical text of Ecclesiastes in Ethiopic, but since none of the manuscripts in Europe was dated earlier than the fifteenth century he determined to visit Abyssinia. Armed with a letter of introduction from the archbishop of Canterbury he arrived there in February 1930 and stayed for ten weeks. On one of his field trips from Addis Ababa he discovered a fourteenth-century manuscript of Ecclesiastes, which he photocopied, along with a variety of other documents.[51] The key to his researches was the support of the empress Zauditu ("I have not yet proposed to the Empress," Mercer reported to Provost Cosgrave, "but I have done almost everything else.") The empress, leader of the church party and just three years older than Mercer, died before Mercer left the country, but he had also won the friendship of her enemy, the regent, who now became "King of Kings" with the title of Haile Selassi. Mercer was decorated by the new emperor and was convinced the way was clear to return for a full-scale search of the documentary resources of the country "by younger and stronger men" who would uncover a treasure trove of biblical manuscripts.[52]

For some years before his visit to Ethiopia, Mercer had been interested also in translating the Tell el Amarna tablets, and during the thirties he

[49] *Mail*, 11 April 1921.
[50] *Globe and Mail*, 3 January 1969.
[51] *Aethiops* 3, no. 3 (July 1930–) 33–35.
[52] TCA, Staff Records, Mercer file, S. A. B. Mercer to F. H. Cosgrave, 3 March 1930.

managed, with generous financial help from Cosgrave and friends and admirers, to spend several months each year pursuing this interest. In 1931 he reported, "I visited by auto, donkey or on foot every site in Palestine & Syria in any way associated with the Tell-el Amarna period."[53] Succeeding summers he visited, in more comfort, the libraries and archives of Paris and Munich, always to do last-minute research on footnotes for a promised book and totally oblivious or indifferent to Nazi policies and the deteriorating international situation.

In addition to the losses and gains in personnel already noted in the field of biblical studies, Queen's Theological College added Harry Arnold Kent, "the Sergeant-Major," previously at Pine Hill and Dalhousie, as principal and professor of Semitic languages and Old Testament criticism in 1926, and Nathaniel Micklem in New Testament literature from 1927 to 1931. Samuel MacLean Gilmour, a Manitoban with German training and later a Ph.D. from Chicago, came to Queen's in 1931 to teach New Testament although his specialty was Hebrew. Gilmour made his mark in subsequent years as a scholar and as a social critic. John Henry Riddell, better known to Canadian church historians for his writing on Methodism in the Prairie provinces, was actually a New Testament scholar who had been principal of Alberta Theological College from 1912 to 1918 when he was appointed to Wesley College, Winnipeg, where he taught New Testament exegesis and Oriental languages and literature until 1938.

Two expatriate Canadians who made significant contributions to biblical studies in quite different ways were James D. Smart and T. Cuyler Young. Smart, a graduate of University and Knox colleges, had studied at Marburg, had been a teaching fellow in University College, and after a number of years in the working ministry of the Presbyterian church followed that well-worn southward academic path so familiar to aspiring Canadians to find employment at Union Theological Seminary and recognition for his numerous publications, mainly in biblical theology. By contrast Young, whose background was in American mission work in Iran, taught Oriental languages at Victoria for four years before being seconded to Washington in 1943 for intelligence work. When Young returned to Victoria at the end of the war he introduced a new dimension to biblical studies in Canada by offering Persian for the first time.

At Wycliffe College a familiar face had reappeared at the end of World War I when Henry Venn Pilcher was reappointed in Old Testament in 1919. Pilcher did not publish but was well known locally for his musical abilities, including guest appearances with the Symphony Orchestra and composing the official anthem for Toronto's centenary in 1934. He took over New Testament teaching in 1932 when B. W. Horan left briefly, but he resigned four years later to become coadjutor bishop of Sydney, Australia.

[53] Ibid., Mercer to Cosgrave, 24 March 1931.

Horan returned to Wycliffe after only a year's absence and took up Pilcher's duties in Old Testament but reverted to New Testament in 1944 for five years until he retired. During the forties Horan contributed two articles to *Wycliffe College Studies*. Upon Pilcher's departure in 1936 the college acquired F. D. Coggan, later archbishop of Canterbury, in New Testament, and Geoffrey Parke-Taylor replaced Horan in Old Testament when Horan made his second entry into New Testament. Both became active members of the CSBS. During his years in Toronto, Coggan published five pamphlets and books, but none of them was really an item of research.

During the depression and war years the Canadian community of biblical scholars lost several of its senior members through death. J. F. McLaughlin died in 1933, two years after retirement, and McCurdy followed him in 1935. At McCurdy's funeral (conducted by three of his most distinguished students, Taylor, Eakin, and Davidson) W. R. Taylor eulogized the founder of Canadian biblical studies as "a Christian humanist"—"his point of view at all times . . . was consistently Christian, [and] his broad interests so raised him above narrow conceptions of religion that there was nothing in the concerns of men that was foreign to him."[54] One year after McCurdy, George Coulton Workman was gone—a minute of the CSBS recorded "his tenacious adherence to views which were supposed to be subversive and destructive."[55] W. G. Jordan, who had been hailed as "Queen's ablest professor"[56] died in 1939, ten years after his retirement, and Sir Robert Falconer and Richard Davidson passed on in November 1943 and May 1944, marking the end of a generation who had taught and fought for biblical criticism, occasionally by confrontation but most often by "a sane and tactful course."

[54] UChA, Printed Order of Service for the funeral of J. F. McCurdy, unpaged.
[55] CSBS Records, file 2, minutes, 1936.
[56] H. J. Morgan, *The Canadian Men and Women of the Time*, 2d ed. (Toronto: William Briggs, 1912) p. 594.

IV

NO MEAN PLACE

Near Eastern Studies have occupied no mean place in the Canadian scene, but one could wish that there might be more research, spread over a wider area.

Theophile James Meek, 1958

Canadian Roman Catholics and Biblical Scholarship

One event of immeasurable importance to biblical studies occurred during World War II—and passed almost unnoticed in most sectors of the scholarly community. On 30 September 1943, the feast day of St. Jerome, Pius XII issued the encyclical *Divino Afflante Spiritu,* which invited, even urged, Roman Catholic scholars to enter fully into the field of biblical studies. Since the Reformation and particularly since the Council of Trent, the Roman Catholic church had officially espoused and enforced a conservative and literalist approach to the Bible, an approach that persisted and was reinforced in reaction to the development of biblical studies by Protestants and rabbinical students and to "modernism" and "liberalism" among Roman Catholics.

The beginning of critical biblical studies among Roman Catholics can be dated from Leo XIII's encyclical *Providentissimus Deus* (1893), which offered a schema for biblical studies when undertaken by trained and reliable teachers and when based predominantly on the "authentic" Vulgate version. If this letter opened the way to biblical research for Roman Catholics, scholars were simultaneously warned that biblical texts must still be interpreted in conformity with a sense determined by the church or supported unanimously by the Fathers in their writings. The study of Oriental languages and the art of scientific criticism might be encouraged, but Leo warned against the pitfalls of "higher criticism" and reaffirmed the inerrancy of scripture.

A subsequent encyclical, from Pius X in 1907, refuted erroneous teaching by "Modernists" or liberals by an antihistorical approach to the issues of inerrancy, inspiration, and authorship of the scriptures. The importance of *Divino Afflante Spiritu* was that it "implicitly revoked"[1] the conservative

---

[1] R. E. Brown, J. A. Fitzmyer, and R. E. Murphy, eds., *The Jerome Biblical Commentary* (Englewood Cliffs, NJ: Prentice-Hall, 1968) vol 2, p. 629, §25.

restrictions of the earlier decrees, approved the distinction of literary forms in the scriptures, encouraged the study of the works of the Church Fathers, disclaimed inerrancy (but not infallibility) in the Vulgate and, finally, urged Roman Catholic scholars to tackle unsolved biblical problems. This last policy was "a refreshing change from the atmosphere after the Modernist crisis when Catholic exegetes deliberately sought 'safe' areas for their biblical research."[2]

One evidence of this expanded Roman Catholic interest and activity in biblical studies was the publication of *La Bible de Jérusalem* in 1956 based on the research and earlier publications of l'École biblique, the Dominican biblical school in Jerusalem. Ten years later the English translation, *The Jerusalem Bible*, was issued, but in neither instance were Canadian scholars directly involved. Roman Catholic authorities who considered the biblical school at Jerusalem to be too radical in its biblical interpretation had founded in 1909 as a counterweight the Pontifical Biblical Institute in Rome under Jesuit direction. It is noteworthy that most Canadian and other Roman Catholic biblical students went to the conservative institute until the liberalizing influence of *Divino Afflante Spiritu* was felt. That encyclical was in fact written for Pius XII by the then rector of the institute, Augustin Bea, later Cardinal Bea. Canadian francophone scholars, nevertheless, were more likely to be affected by the liberal tradition of the Dominican school in Jerusalem, and after World War II were also well acquainted with current biblical literature in English and German periodicals.[3]

Among English-speaking Roman Catholics the next milestone in the development of biblical studies was the appearance in 1968 of the *Jerome Biblical Commentary*. Remarking on North America's role in this general development Augustin Cardinal Bea pointed to the establishment of the Catholic Biblical Association and its *Catholic Biblical Quarterly* and concluded, "The present commentary on the whole Bible is another instance of this spirit."[4] "It is no secret," added the editors of the *Commentary*, "that the last fifteen or twenty years have seen almost a revolution in Catholic biblical studies—a revolution encouraged by authority, for its Magna Carta was the encyclical *Divino Afflante Spiritu* (1943) of Pope Pius XII. The principles of literary and historical criticism, so long regarded with suspicion, are now, at last, accepted and applied by Catholic exegetes. The results have been many. . . ."[5] Among the fifty contributors to the *Commentary* were six Canadians—R. A. F. MacKenzie, David Stanley, J. T. Forestell, Ignatius Hunt, J. L. D'Aragon and Guy P. Couturier, the last two from the Université de Montréal.

[2] Ibid., §23.
[3] Private information from Rev. Père Adrien Brunet.
[4] *Jerome Biblical Commentary*, vol. 1, p. vii.
[5] Ibid., p. xvii.

MacKenzie, the most distinguished anglophone Canadian Roman Catholic scholar in the field and author of books and articles on both Old and New Testament, was at the time rector of the Pontifical Biblical Institute in Rome. He had taught Old Testament at Regis College, Toronto, for fourteen years, had served as president of the Catholic Biblical Association of America and of the International Organization for Old Testament Studies, had been a consultant at Vatican II and to the Pontifical Biblical Commission, and subsequently was general editor of *Biblica* and *Biblia Ecumenica Española*. David Stanley had published several books and articles in New Testament studies and, like his fellow Jesuit MacKenzie, had been president of the Catholic Biblical Association (they are the only Canadians elected to that office to date), and had been a member of the New Testament Translation Board for the New American Bible and with Frank W. Beare had been the second Canadian on the Standard Bible Committee.

The Jerusalem Bible (English version) and the *Jerome Biblical Commentary* both appeared soon after a major statement by the second Vatican Council on the subject of biblical studies. *Instructio de Historia Evangeliorum Veritate* was issued in April 1964, and the following year the *Canadian Journal of Theology* carried an article on the *Instructio* by Beare. Beare believed that the document supported "the widest liberty of scholarly investigation, and asks only that it should be exercised in a spirit of responsibility."[6] Noting the way that recent Roman Catholic experience with biblical studies had been telescoped in a short time (in contrast to the long development of the discipline in Protestant circles), he commented on how the "extraordinary outburst of activity among biblical scholars of the Roman Catholic Church" following *Divino Afflante Spiritu* had produced a generation of scholarly research that was "nothing short of magnificent. . . . The massive learning . . . has been matched by a boldness and freedom that is hardly to be equalled anywhere, and certainly not to be surpassed."[7]

One purely Canadian undertaking that flowed from these scholarly biblical interests was Paul-Émile Langevin's compilation and publication in 1972 of *Bibliographie Biblique*, a systematic analysis of seventy Roman Catholic journals covering the years 1930–70. A second volume not only brought the bibliography down chronologically to 1975 but provided analyses of over eight hundred books and added fifty more journals published in French, English, German, Italian, and Spanish. The results of this labor, amounting to over twenty-five hundred pages in print, were published by Les Presses de l'Université Laval with the text in all five languages.

For francophone Canadian biblical scholars, the issuing of *Divino Afflante Spiritu* coincided with a project of Fides publishers in Montreal to

---

[6] F. W. Beare, "The Historical Truth of the Gospels: An Official Pronouncement of the Pontifical Biblical Commission," *CJT* 11 (1965) 232.

[7] Ibid., p. 231.

produce a French-text New Testament translated from Greek. In 1944 the team of translators formed the nucleus of l'Association catholique des études bibliques au Canada (ACEBAC), the French-speaking scholarly biblical society in Canada and in North America. Its annual meetings were normally held in the province of Quebec, but four of its first fifteen meetings did occur outside that province—at Ottawa, London and Sudbury in Ontario, and at Edmunston, New Brunswick. ACEBAC's programs, most often exegetical in emphasis, became highly thematic after the first few years. Although working within the Roman Catholic tradition of interpretation, the society never felt any constraint on freedom of inquiry despite the existence within French-Canadian Roman Catholicism of persons and groups who mirrored the literalism of some Protestants in an earlier generation. "Le but de l'ACEBAC n'est ni spirituelle, ni pastoral, ni apologétique, mais toujours rigoureusement scientifique. . . ."[8]

The membership of ACEBAC was about seventy, only slightly smaller than that of the CSBS. "Malgré son caractère catholique," wrote the secretary of ACEBAC in 1970,

> l'ACEBAC ne fait pas une étude 'confessionnelle' des textes bibliques. On fait peut-être difficilement de l'exégèse sans préjugés, mais l'ACEBAC ose l'entreprendre. C'est ce qui rend possibles ses rapports avec des organismes protestants ou non confessionels comme la Society of Biblical Literature (USA) et la Canadian Society of Biblical Studies (Canada), dont un membre de l'ACEBAC, le Père Adrien Brunet, o.p., a déjà été le président. Si la collaboration n'est pas aussi régulière et soutenue que l'ACEBAC le souhaitrait, c'est à cause de la barrière linguistique créée par l'ignorance du français chez trop de biblistes anglophones du Canada et des États-Unis.[9]

In its first two decades ACEBAC expanded its contacts with other biblical studies groups such as the Catholic Biblical Association, the Canadian Theological Society, and the CSBS. About 1960 the association began to hold semiannual regional meetings, and at the same time the need for biblical documentary materials led ACEBAC to establish a library that would supplement but not duplicate existing resources, either institutional or private; in the space of a decade a circulating collection of some two thousand volumes was assembled. For the Canadian francophone community of biblical scholars ACEBAC has created and maintained in its members a strong sense of purpose and unity and a focus for contacts both national and international. If language and confession give ACEBAC some greater degree of cohesion than the Canadian Society of Biblical Studies enjoys, ACEBAC also possesses a certain financial security since it continues to share in the publisher's profits from the French New Testament version that was the historic seed-bed for the creation of the association.

---

[8] "ACEBAC," *Religiologiques*, Les Cahiers de l'Université du Québec, 1970, p. 171.
[9] Ibid., pp. 170–71.

Roman Catholic involvement in the CSBS began when the Dominican scholar Adrien Brunet, who had pioneered in this field among Canadian francophones, joined the society in 1954 and delivered a paper at that year's meeting. Commenting on Brunet's contribution, Frank Beare expressed regret that the paper had not been read in French. The following year two more Roman Catholic scholars, David Stanley and R. A. F. MacKenzie, both Jesuits, joined the CSBS. In 1958 Stanley was elected president and in 1964 Brunet became the society's first francophone president. This expansion of the CSBS into a bilingual and interdenominational organization within a generation after *Divino Afflante Spiritu* reflected the growth of Roman Catholic biblical scholarship. The CSBS and ACEBAC have never met jointly, but CSBS representatives have attended ACEBAC conferences.

While Quebec's "Quiet Revolution" of the 1960s was most apparent in its political and social aspects, of equal if not greater importance was its educational revolution, which predated and in ways provoked the Quiet Revolution. The educational revolution in turn had an impact on biblical scholars, especially as a system that had been completely confessional was "secularized" almost overnight and new departments of religious studies were built from its traditional theological and philosophical foundations. Writing in the preface to the 1972 edition of C. P. Anderson's survey of religious teaching in Canadian universities, Michel-M. Campbell commented on "l'étrange et complexe dialectique" in Canada's francophone community apparent in the trend to secularization on the one hand and in continuing interest in religious studies on the other. He found this situation quite different from that in anglophone Canada; among francophones the intellectual climate continued to be more monolithic and conservative. In the midst of the growth of religious studies the distinctiveness of disciplines was being preserved and no attempt was being made there to answer the question plaguing Europeans and anglophone North Americans—whether religious studies was a discrete subject.[10]

Among Canada's francophone universities Laval at Quebec City, Moncton in New Brunswick, Montréal and the Université de Québec à Montréal (UQAM) developed religious studies programs but the Université de Montréal was apparently the only one of these to offer advanced work in religious studies to the Ph.D. level and, interestingly, was the only Canadian university to give doctorates specifically in "Biblical Studies." Parallel to this institutional growth was the achievement of both national and international recognition of francophone biblical scholars. A generation after *Divino Afflante Spiritu* Frank Beare had hailed the growth of Roman Catholic biblical scholarship as "nothing short of magnificent."[11] Two generations

[10] C. P. Anderson, *Guide to Religious Studies in Canada*, 3d ed. (Corporation for the Publication of Academic Studies of Religion in Canada, 1972) pp. 32–33.

[11] Beare, "Historical Truth," p. 231.

after the promulgation of that encyclical those scholars bid fair to outstrip their non-Catholic colleagues who started with the advantage of a century of biblical studies behind them.

Changes in the Canadian Society of Biblical Studies

For the first two decades of its existence the CSBS had met at one or other of the colleges in Toronto but never, surprisingly, at University College. Toronto was the central and sensible location for the meetings because of the high proportion of Canadian biblical scholars resident there or within reasonable traveling distance. In 1953, however, this pattern was changed as the society gathered at Queen's University, Kingston, and three years later the meetings were held in Montreal at McGill. Thereafter and throughout the sixties Toronto was only occasionally the host city. During the war years the society underwent several small but important changes. The membership declined to about seventy, but a high proportion paid their dues and the financial situation improved markedly. Among its members the society now had a considerable number of rabbis. The mimeographed *Bulletin* had proved its worth and its economy—125 copies cost less than nine dollars. Having survived the exigencies of the war and the loss of both Falconer and Davidson, the society greeted the postwar period with optimism.

Responding to the growing interest in biblical theology, John Dow of Emmanuel College proposed in 1945 "that the basis of the Society be broadened, so that theological interests, other than those exclusively biblical, might be represented in both its membership and in the annual presentation of papers."[12] After consideration of this resolution the executive announced that its intention was already within the purview of the society, thanks to the terms of the constitution, and recommended that in future programs one session "be reserved for the less technical papers," those not of a literary or historical character. The meeting of 1946 approved this plan and the following year Dow's presidential address was entitled "Some trends of Biblical Theology from E. Renan onwards." This was the only theological paper on that year's program, but David Hay and Rabbi H. A. Fischel were elected to the executive. At the same time a unique arrangement occurred—Fischel was elected president of the SBL branch but Kenneth Evans became president of the CSBS. The rapprochement of biblical studies and biblical theology continued with papers in 1951 from two prominent theologians, Eugene Fairweather and David Hay, who was the current president.

Further broadening of the society's bases came with the decision in 1949 to have one member (in this case S. M. Gilmour) represent the CSBS at

---

[12] CSBS, minutes, 1945; see B. S. Childs (*Biblical Theology in Crisis* [Philadelphia: Westminster, 1970] p. 21) for a reference to Presbyterian influences and to James D. Smart.

the meetings of the forty-year-old National Association of Biblical Instructors. To the same end of enlarging the society's interests and numbers, several campaigns were undertaken to involve more persons from the ranks of the "working clergy." Although local "working clergy" did attend meetings as visitors, membership totals suggest that, for whatever reason, they did not join and support the CSBS. By the mid-fifties membership and participation had been broadened to include Roman Catholic biblical scholars, both French- and English-speaking, yet at the same time the number of rabbis who belonged to the society had shrunk to one—Harry Stern of Montreal, who would class himself among the "working clergy" rather than among the "scholars" but supported the CSBS because he believed such organizations promoted Canadian unity. This decline of Jewish membership undoubtedly mirrored the strong conservative trend in rabbinical studies that developed after the establishment of the state of Israel. Nevertheless the general broadening process continued into the late 1950s as church historians joined the society, thus paving the way for the subsequent organization of joint meetings of the CSBS with the Canadian Theological Society and the Canadian Society of Church History.

The programs of the CSBS meetings during the fifties also reflected this broadening of interests to fields other than biblical theology. In addition to hearing papers from the new Roman Catholic members, the substance of the program ranged more widely than in past years. In 1956 John Wevers spoke as president on the Dead Sea Scrolls and New Testament Studies, and at the following meeting Gerald Harrop discussed the reissue in paperback of one of Wellhausen's classics, a publishing trend that had also recently reproduced works by S. R. Driver and Robertson Smith. Within another three years a Canadian classic—T. J. Meek's *Hebrew Origins*—also appeared in the "new clothes," as Harrop described it, of a paperback edition.

By the early 1960s the CSBS was consciously approaching a crossroad that would decisively influence the future development of biblical studies in Canada. At the 1960 meeting Frank Beare commented on how the society had grown into a national institution representative of the various regions, of both English- and French-speaking Canadian biblical scholars, of Roman Catholic and Protestant communities, and of "collegians" and parish ministers. The following year the Canadian Theological Society and the Canadian Society of Church History coordinated their meetings at McGill with the meeting of the CSBS and arranged joint sessions to hear the presidential addresses of the three societies. Although the attendance had been disappointing, the McGill meetings were pronounced a resounding success because for the first time three organizations with cognate interests in religion had met at a professional and social level. Undoubtedly the prior existence of an overlapping membership in the societies contributed to this ease of association.

Perhaps those very achievements of the 1961 meeting required that the three societies examine their relationship to each other and, equally important, their individual relationships to all the other Canadian scholarly societies. These societies, meeting annually at different locations under the aegis of the Royal Society of Canada, constituted the Learned Societies, or more popularly, "the Learneds." A discussion of these relationships occurred separately in each of the three "Learned Religious Societies" when they gathered at Wycliffe College in May 1962. In the CSBS Stewart McCullough and Robert Lennox moved that the society maintain its separate identity (the minutes do not indicate a vote on the resolution), and McCullough and Norman E. Wagner were appointed a committee to investigate the possibility of regional meetings of the CSBS—in the Maritimes, in the central provinces, and in the West. At the same time a tri-society committee was charged to report the next year on the future relations of the "religious learneds."

Unfortunately neither minutes nor *Bulletin* exists for 1963, but the records of the Canadian Society of Church History show that a proposal for a single society of religious studies had been examined and rejected by the tripartite committee, "in large part because the historians were satisfied with the existing arrangements."[13] At this point the question of relationship to the "Learneds" was shelved but not forgotten. Developments in the Canadian scholarly community dictated that the issue would of necessity be reopened and resolved before the decade ended, but for the moment the collective meetings of the three societies (membership in one conferred honorary membership without privileges in the others) and the joint sessions for presidential papers and social activities continued to give general satisfaction.

With the return of peace in 1945 the format of the *Bulletin* changed and its size was reduced from some thirty pages to about a dozen. Thereafter for more than a decade the contents of the *Bulletin* consisted of the presidential address in full, summaries of other papers, and an account of proceedings at the previous meeting of the society. In 1958 no papers or synopses were printed; G. B. Caird's presidential address appeared in the *Canadian Journal of Theology*. After 1959 the *Bulletin* was suspended for four years, perhaps because the new *Canadian Journal of Theology* was providing a wider audience for major papers in the biblical field. In the early sixties, however, an infusion of younger and enthusiastic members led to the revival of the *Bulletin* under the editorship of Norman Wagner, newly elected to the office of secretary-treasurer. To mark the centenary of Canadian confederation in 1967 Wagner designed a special mimeographed volume containing six "key" presidential papers, "not only [to] pay respect to the scholars of the past, but also [to] permit the younger scholars among us to become acquainted with our predecessors. . . ."[14] The first paper was an

[13] J. S. Moir, "The Canadian Society of Church History—a twenty-year retrospect," *The Canadian Society of Church History, Papers 1980*, p. 83.

[14] *Canadian Biblical Studies, 1967*, p. 11.

updated version of John Macpherson's 1962 presidential address surveying the development of the society. Fittingly, R. B. Y. Scott, the society's first secretary-treasurer, penned "a word of greeting," complimenting the society on past achievements and its "new vigour" of recent years.[15]

When Wagner resigned as secretary-treasurer in favor of Robert C. Culley in 1969, further changes were introduced into the *Bulletin*. Its size almost doubled—a reflection of the quantitative growth of scholarly activity in the field—and a section headed "Society Activities: News Items," carrying valuable bibliographic information on members' publications, was added. Culley, based in Montreal, was particularly aware of the work of Canadian francophone scholars. In 1972 the society adopted the name "Canadian Society of Biblical Studies/Société canadienne des études bibliques" and the acronym CSBS/SCEB. Three years later the *Bulletin* carried for the first time papers in French, by the president André Legault and by the prize-winning essayist of that year, Simon Dufour. As early as the mid-fifties bilingual notices had been used by the society occasionally, but after 1970 this became a regular practice, although the minutes still were kept in English only.

In the late sixties the question of the society's relation to the Learneds was reopened. Members were now convinced that the CSBS must win recognition as a "learned" society and much time was spent by the executive discussing qualification with the Canada Council which, as the provider of financial support for the various Learneds, was the public arbiter in such matters. The popular misconception of the CSBS as a "ministerial association"[16] was successfully dispelled by the arguments of the president, Robert Osborne, who pointed to the age of the society and to the academic prestige of "our distinguished founders—Sir R[obert] Falconer, Dr. R. B. Y. Scott, etc." In 1971 the society was in fact acknowledged to be "learned," as were its sister societies, the Canadian Theological Society and the Canadian Society of Church History. The Canadian Society for the Study of Religion had already been accepted into the Learneds when the CSSR was founded in the late sixties.

Once the link with the Learneds was complete the question of joint programming with the two other religious learned societies had to be faced. Where previously their common interest in religion had drawn the three together, they now found their loyalties torn by their proximity to other cognate societies such as the Canadian Society for Studies in Religion (CSSR) and the Canadian Historical Association, who did not meet concurrently. A valiant effort was made by all parties to schedule related programs within a restricted period but the historians drifted away from old friends toward the Canadian Historical Association and the Canadian Catholic Historical

[15] Ibid., p. iv.
[16] Private information from Robert Osborne, 19 March 1979.

Association. The joint sessions to hear the presidential papers of the three societies had already become less frequently attended even before the staggered scheduling was accepted.[17]

Even while the relations of the CSBS to the Learneds were being discussed in 1969, the society was also involved in a reappraisal of its relationship to the SBL (the phrase "and Exegesis" had been dropped from its name in 1962). The changes that followed in Canada occurred partially independently and partially in response to the many-faceted developments that followed in the older organization. In 1968 the new executive secretary of the SBL, Robert W. Funk, had proposed a wide variety of alterations in that society's structure and functions, including "decentralization by the strengthening of Sections."[18] A year later the society accepted these extensive innovations at its one hundred and fifth meeting, held in Toronto. In the restructuring of sections (increased to ten), the CSBS was consulted because of its peculiar status, being nearly coterminous with the Canadian Section of the SBL. Writing to Robert Funk, the CSBS secretary, Robert C. Culley, commented, "As for our dual role no one seems unhappy about it,"[19] to which Funk replied, "I see no real problems with the current set-up in Canada, so long as it works for you."[20]

At the same time the CSBS secretary sent a memo to members of both Canadian groups asking whether their organization should be national or regional, what the implications of the dual role would be, and if a council should be formed from all the Canadian societies interested in religion along the lines of the American Council on the Study of Religion. As part of its response to the growing specialization of the interests of its members, the society considered the following year a plan to organize study groups on such themes as interpretation, Samaritan studies, Ugaritic studies, and the Hebrew Bible. The first of these interest groups to start functioning was for Ugaritic, soon followed by text criticism. In 1975 the Ugaritic group began to issue its own *Newsletter*, edited by Peter Craigie. This practice was adopted by other interest groups as they got established, but the Ugaritic *Newsletter* has been the most successful and is known internationally.

By 1972 the CSBS membership stood at 88, but the Canadian SBL branch had 127 members. Two years later the CSBS's membership had declined, but over one hundred belonged to the SBL. Membership figures for the CSBS continued to fluctuate but showed a long-term decline, while the SBL figures continued to rise slightly. This trend inevitably raised again the question of regional versus nationwide structures. As a result of the

---

[17] Moir, "Canadian Society of Church History," p. 81.

[18] E. W. Saunders, "A Century of Service to American Biblical Scholarship," *Bulletin of the Council on the Study of Religion* 11 (1980) 71.

[19] CSBS Papers, File 5, R. C. Culley to R. W. Funk, 12 May 1970.

[20] Ibid., R. W. Funk to R. C. Culley, 20 May 1970.

regionalization of the American SBL branches Canadian members found it more advantageous in many ways to work within the nearest American branch, rather than try to maintain a separate national branch for so few members separated by such a long distance. Within a short time Canadian scholars became actively involved in the Eastern Great Lakes, the Midwest, the Eastern International, and the Pacific Northwest regions of the SBL, and the Canadian branch, which had begun on the eve of World War II, ceased to operate in 1977. Within the SBL Central organization many Canadians have served in executive capacities, and at least seven have been elected to the office of president, five of them in the period 1958-70—S. J. Case in 1926, T. J. Meek in 1944, W. A. Irwin in 1958, R. B. Y. Scott in 1960, F. V. Winnett in 1964, F. W. Beare in 1969 (when the SBL held its meetings in Toronto), and Harry Orlinsky in 1970.

The CSBS's membership has risen quickly in recent years (to 165 in 1981), and its composition reflects significant changes of interest. At the society's inauguration members had been drawn from the faculties of universities (some with denominational connections) and Protestant theological colleges and from the "working clergy," including the four rabbis. The immediate postwar years were notable, however, for the arrival of several biblical theologians and the first Roman Catholic members, both French- and English-speaking, and for proportionate decline of Jewish interest. Since the 1960s the membership of the CSBS has become more cosmopolitan as Canadian universities attracted—and retained—faculty from the United States, from Great Britain, and from Germany. Today the majority of the CSBS members are employed in departments of religion rather than in theological colleges as was the case when the society was formed. Two further changes in membership became evident during the 1970s. The academic element in the membership continued to increase as in most Canadian learned societies at the expense of what might be called the "general interest" group. At the same time, however, the society is attracting scholars from a wider academic spectrum including English, philosophy, classics, and of course the burgeoning field of religious studies. The presence of these new interests virtually calls for a redefinition of "biblical studies" to include not merely the traditional fields of Near Eastern languages, literature, history, and archeology, but also such cognate fields as English Bible studies, biblical ethics, and even computer science.

As with other disciplines in Canada since World War II, biblical studies have become more uniformly interested in research and publishing. The wide range of notable biblical research activities undertaken in Canada in recent years includes the McMaster University project on "Normative Self-Definition of Judaism and Christianity," funded for five years by the Social Science and Humanities Research Council of Canada; important Septuagint studies at the Université de Sherbrooke and by John Wevers at the University of Toronto; the computer-assisted research related to Targumic studies carried on by John Hurd, Walter Aufrecht, and Ernest Clarke in Toronto and by Lloyd Gaston in Vancouver; and the planned cooperative two volumes of essays in the Anti-Judaism Project headed by Peter Richardson of University College and David Granskou of Wilfrid Laurier University. At the same time Canadians have hosted international meetings of scholars in the biblical and related fields—the SBL in Toronto in 1969, the Studiorum Novi Testamenti in the same city in 1980, and the International Association for the History of Religions in Winnipeg in 1980.

Programs at the annual meetings of the CSBS reflect these varied changes in the discipline. Program content over the years has improved both in quantity and in quality. The 1981 meetings, as an example, offered a total of thirty-two papers, half in Old Testament, half in New. Speakers are now drawn from a more varied group of participants representing diverse interests, and the meetings also serve as a showcase for young and promising scholars. The society's system of awards for outstanding research papers by students is integrated into the annual program through having the winning essays presented orally by their authors. In sum, in terms of variety of interests, scope of individual and group research projects, publications, and programming, biblical studies in Canada now present new and exciting prospects which the founders of the CSBS could not have imagined a half century earlier.

A second professional group involving Canadian biblical scholars, the Toronto Oriental Club, was formed in 1952 on the initiative of John W. Wevers with the support of Gilbert Bagnani of University College's classics department. Wevers had belonged to the Philadelphia Oriental Club before moving to Toronto in 1951, and the Toronto group was consciously modeled on that in Philadelphia. Some twenty scholars interested in the Oriental world in the broadest sense formed the original membership and elected T. J. Meek as president, Bagnani as vice-president and Wevers as secretary-treasurer. Thereafter membership has been limited to fifty persons chosen by nomination and election. Members, and infrequently nonmembers, present scientific papers at the club's four yearly meetings, and a collection of these papers by members was published under the title *The Seed of Wisdom* (1964) in honor of T. J. Meek.[21] Another Festschrift, involving several members of the Toronto Oriental Club but produced under other auspices, was entitled *Studies in the Ancient Palestinian World* and was presented to Fred V. Winnett in 1971.

Biblical Studies and Religious Studies

In the late 1950s and early 1960s two developments within Canadian universities affected biblical studies in different but related ways. The first

---

[21] Private information of John W. Wevers.

was the introduction of modern Near Eastern language studies—modern
Hebrew, Arabic, Persian, Turkish, and Urdu. Although classical Hebrew,
Arabic, and Syriac were still taught by the departments of Oriental languages and literature and in theological colleges, interrelationships both
academic and personal inevitably grew up between the two related fields.[22]
The second development—the creation of university faculties or departments of religious studies—had more obvious impact on biblical studies in
terms of organizational structures, curricular changes, and student interest
and must be seen against the background of such bewildering contemporary
developments as Vatican II, the crisis of faith, the loss of authority, and the
rise of countercultures.

As late as the mid-sixties most Canadian Catholic colleges and universities as well as Acadia, and Trinity and Victoria at Toronto, prescribed
courses in religion or theology as partial requirements for a bachelor's
degree, although only half of them offered major programs in religion or
theology. Paradoxically this requirement was abandoned by virtually every
one of these institutions at the very time that departments of religion were
being established. In a few other universities religion courses were not
required but could, to an established maximum, be counted as credits
toward the B.A.[23] "The main breakthrough was the acceptance by the
university community of a distinction between the religious study of religion
and its secular study. This important distinction was the ideological prerequisite for the founding or evolution of several new departments of
religious studies [e.g. at McMaster, Sir George Williams, and the University
of British Columbia] around 1960. . . . By the mid-1960's . . . the concept of
religious studies as a reputable academic enterprise had been widely
accepted in the university, despite some pockets of resistance."[24]

"From divinity to religious studies"—the phrase is not simply a statement
of a transmutation but of an expansion of role and change of direction for
biblical studies in Canada that occurred during the two decades after World
War II. Obviously theology did not disappear as an academic program but
much of it, including biblical studies, was remolded and offered in the arts
faculties of Canadian universities under the aegis of departments of religion,
which mushroomed in number and attractiveness during the period. The large
number of students entering the new programs, which included ethics,
psychology of religion, sociology of religion, and studies in various aspects of
Near and Far Eastern civilizations, was proof that "the academic study of
religion [has become] a subject intended for others than ordinands."[25]

---

[22] R. S. Harris, A History of Higher Education in Canada 1663–1960 (Toronto: University of
Toronto Press, [1976]) p. 517.

[23] Anderson, Guide to Religious Studies, p. 8.

[24] Ibid., pp. 8, 9.

[25] J. C. McLelland, "From Divinity to Religious Studies: '48–'78," Arc 6, no. 1 (Autumn 1978).

In 1967 C. P. Anderson and T. A. Nosanchuk, responding to the interest in academic religious studies, compiled *The 1967 Guide to Religious Studies in Canada* using material from the calendars of the various universities. Two years later, when a new and more drastically expanded analytic edition of the *Guide* appeared, Anderson noted in the preface, "The 1967 edition of this Guide was not yet completed when it became apparent that the rapid development of religious studies in Canada would soon necessitate a new edition."[26] This edition was in turn replaced by a third in 1972, which in addition to updated curricular information from the universities contained much statistical data and two useful essays—by Anderson and Michel Campbell—on the changes in religious studies in English-speaking and in French-speaking institutions from 1967 to 1972.

In that five-year period the number of courses offered in English-speaking universities rose by 150 percent, from 180 to 450. At the same time seven departments or faculties had changed their titles from "theology" or "divinity" to "religious studies." In 1967 the theological and religious departments had employed a total of 140 faculty members; in 1972 that number stood at 220. The decision in 1968 to combine the college departments of religion at the University of Toronto into a single department had created the largest group of its kind in Canada, with thirty-one faculty members in 1972. Whereas in 1967 45 percent of the faculty in the field of religious studies had earned doctorates, that percentage had risen to 70 in 1972, at which date 70 percent of all English or bilingual Canadian universities were offering major programs in religious studies.

While the secular universities had a certain advantage in this development inasmuch as they could design programs without any preconditions or influences inherited from a previous denominational connection, those older institutions that had begun in the nineteenth century as church-related colleges often had the advantage of being able to draw personnel and content from already established faculties of theology and courses of religious knowledge. United College (renamed the University of Winnipeg), for instance, transformed its Faculty of Theology into a Department of Religious Studies in 1966. In the case of Concordia in Montreal (created in 1974 by the merging of the Jesuit college, Loyola, and the YMCA institution, Sir George Williams) a program of theological studies that embraced biblical studies and employed non-Catholic instructors had already been developed at Loyola before it merged with the secularly based Sir George Williams and its program of religious studies, which included the M.A. in Judaic studies. In this case the merged institutions adopted a unique solution—to retain both the Department of Theological Studies at Loyola in the Faculty of Arts and the Department of Religious Studies of Sir George in the Faculty of Social Sciences.

---

[26] *The 1969 Guide to Religious Studies in Canada* (n.p., 1969) preface.

By contrast with these older "religious institutions," one of the earliest universities to develop a strong undergraduate program in religious studies was the secular Carleton University in Ottawa. In the early 1970s Carleton accounted for almost one third of all English-speaking students majoring in religion. After more than a decade of experience Carleton's solid undergraduate program provided a foundation for expansion into graduate work.[27] The "state" University of Calgary was later than its parent institution, the University of Alberta, in entering into religious studies but developed very rapidly both undergraduate and graduate programs in the field, thanks to the pioneer work of Peter Craigie. McMaster, which had been secularized after World War II by separating from McMaster Divinity College, developed a very large and well-funded research program at the graduate level of religious studies.

At McGill, a Faculty of Divinity was created in 1948 within the university, employing three members of the older joint faculty now cross-appointed to be university professors. During the year four more appointments were made to the new faculty, including George B. Caird in New Testament to complement R. B. Y. Scott in Old Testament, and Wilfred Cantwell Smith (comparative religion) who later in 1951–52, established McGill's Institute of Islamic Studies. This organizational change at McGill had been debated at length in the early forties, but it was a proposal in 1947 to offer religious knowledge courses in the Faculty of Arts and Science that precipitated the action.[28] A committee of representatives of McGill and the theological colleges was formed with Scott as its secretary, and when the terms of the arrangement were settled Scott was named dean of the new faculty. At the same time Divinity Hall and its endowment were transferred to the university. With the creation of new degree programs related to religious studies at McGill the name of the faculty of "Divinity" was changed in 1970 to "Religious Studies," "as indicative of the broader interests" being developed within the university, and Divinity Hall was renamed the William Henry Birks Building two years later.[29]

After two decades there were no fewer than thirty departments of religious studies in Canadian universities with undergraduate programs and at least seven—McGill, McMaster, Montréal, Concordia, Ottawa, British Columbia, and Toronto—were offering Ph.D. degrees in religious studies. Doctoral studies in the biblical field were not, however, confined to the new departments of religion. The Toronto, Atlantic, and Vancouver schools of theology and the theological faculties at McGill and Acadia now offer such work with a Th.D. program. With no single institution or country dominating

---

[27] Anderson, *Guide to Religious Studies*, p. 68.

[28] H. K. Markell, *The Faculty of Religious Studies, McGill University, 1948–78* (Montreal: Faculty of Religious Studies, McGill University, 1979) pp. 17–24.

[29] Ibid., pp. 53–54.

graduate biblical studies Canadian universities with these programs attracted their share of the international student body. Similarly, by 1980 only twelve universities in Canada did not offer undergraduate programs in religious studies. Of these at least one—Lethbridge—was developing such a program, and another—King's—had access to the department of Dalhousie University, to which King's is affiliated. Two of these twelve were francophone and previously religious-based, but of the remaining ten anglophone institutions nine were "secular" in origin.

One significant and virtually universal feature of all these new departments of religion was the dominance of the methodology of the social sciences, an inheritance in large measure from the American academic scene and particularly from the University of Chicago, where many younger Canadians had received their graduate training before returning to teach in Canadian universities. This "social science" approach to religion was at variance with the traditional Canadian emphasis on historical methodology especially in the field of biblical studies, where even at the turn of the century the term "historical criticism" had been preferred to "higher criticism," and apparently opposing ideologies created a tension within some departments that continues to surface in a variety of forms.

Writing in 1980 about current North American trends in New Testament studies, E. P. Sanders expressed another concern, that the development of departments of religious studies had exacerbated "the traditional weakness in North American education, a solid grounding in languages and history."[30] The new programs, he believes, have been particularly destructive of language studies because language requirements have been eroded and more often than not eliminated. "It is thus now possible for an undergraduate student to major in religion and to do several courses in New Testament with straight A's . . . without ever learning a word of Greek." Such students are obviously unprepared for graduate biblical studies because "religious studies departments have all too willingly pretended that religion can be studied entirely in English."

Reviewing the development of religious studies in Canada to 1972, Charles P. Anderson noted the heavy and necessary dependence of the area on the preexisting faculties of theology.

> These faculties, especially in universities of Protestant background, had as their main task neither the education of undergraduates, nor the academic study of religion, but the professional training of clergy. It fell to them, however, to supply many of the resources necessary to teach whatever undergraduate courses in religion were included in the university's curriculum. . . . It was normally expected that the only sympathetic treatment of religion on campus would be found in courses given by the department or faculty of theology. On the other side, many university faculty regarded the department

---

[30] E. P. Sanders, "New Testament Studies Today," unpublished paper, p. 17.

of theology with a suspicion frequently fed by fears of clericalism, anti-intellectualism and proselytism."[31]

Whereas offerings of religious courses in the United States had been confined to the private sector because of the American separation of church and state, in Canada no such dichotomy ever developed because historically Canadians rejected state-churchism but accepted religion as an essential component of education at all levels. Hence biblical studies had developed within most Canadian universities without reference to the "public" or denominational character of the institutions. Anderson had noted the understandable emphasis on Christianity in the formation of university programs in religious studies.[32] During the last decade the non-Christian component in religious studies at Canadian institutions has been enlarged both at the undergraduate and graduate levels, but Canada's historical development makes it likely that Christian studies, including biblical studies, will retain a central place in such curricula.

By the mid-1960s, however, faculties of theology in Canada were feeling the impact of the rise of the departments of religion and the decline of enrollments for the ministry. At Mount Allison University, for instance, where theology had been transferred to Pine Hill in Halifax after the church union in 1925, very few courses in religious subjects were offered to undergraduates until the late 1950s when the arrival of new faculty brought curricular changes as well. A Department of Religion was established in 1960 and enrollments in its courses over the next decade averaged 175. Some of these were candidates for the ministry (who alone were offered pre-theology Hebrew courses), but where over one hundred theology students were identified in the student body in 1960, a decade later their number had shrunk to fourteen, with marked effects on the enrollment in religious studies.[33] A survey in the mid-sixties of twenty-three "mainline Protestant" seminaries revealed that 123 full- and part-time staff were teaching only 667 students.[34] By the late seventies, however, this trend had been reversed and several Canadian theological colleges even reported the largest student enrollments in their histories. At the same time both the theological colleges and the departments of religious studies accept the validity of the other's particular approach to biblical studies—the one in a religiously committed setting, the other in a comparative and descriptive fashion. This dichotomy is not reflected within the CSBS, where virtually all members pursue their studies along identical lines.

---

[31] Anderson, *Guide to Religious Studies*, p. 7.

[32] Ibid., p. 11.

[33] A. J. Ebbutt, "History of Department of Religious Studies," report to the board of regents, Mount Allison University, 6 April 1971, 10 pp.

[34] Charles Feilding, "Twenty-three Theological Schools: Aspects of Canadian Theological Education," *CJT* 12 (1966) 229–37.

A related development in ecumenism and religious studies was the formation in 1969 of the Toronto School of Theology, which pooled the resources—human and material—of Emmanuel, Knox, Regis, St. Augustine's Seminary, Trinity, St. Michael's, and Wycliffe colleges, with McMaster Divinity College as an affiliate, to establish cooperation of five different denominations. Of the 221 basic degree courses offered by TST 45 were in biblical studies, and of 108 courses given by the advanced degree division, 22 were in the Old and New Testament areas. The example of TST was followed on both the Atlantic and Pacific coasts—the Atlantic School of Theology was formed in Halifax and Vancouver School of Theology at Vancouver. AST brought together Holy Heart Theological Institute, Pine Hill Divinity Hall, and the Faculty of Divinity of Canada's oldest university, King's College. Of fifty-eight courses offered at AST seventeen were in the biblical field. VST contained only two institutions, Anglican Theological College and Union College of British Columbia. Together they offered twenty-eight biblical courses of a total of seventy.[35]

Offering biblical studies in a different academic context have been the Bible schools and colleges, which began in Canada with the founding of Toronto Bible College in 1894.[36] For more than forty years the Bible classes at TBC were given by Principal John McNicol, a Presbyterian minister, graduate of University and Knox colleges, and a former student of McCurdy, who developed a highly successful and widely imitated Bible study curriculum.[37] After World War I Bible schools and colleges multiplied rapidly in Canada and of over one hundred established by 1980 forty-six were founded in the interwar years (1919–1939) alone, and thirty-five or three-quarters of those were in the three Prairie provinces.[38] One interesting recent development in these institutions has been the trend to seek teachers for the fields of Old and New Testament with postgraduate training and advanced degrees from recognized universities. A further stage in this process has been the creation since World War II of the Institute for Christian Studies at Toronto, which independently offers postgraduate studies within an intellectual climate that attempts to be both conservative and scholarly. Its Christian Reformed tradition is underscored by its affiliation with the Free University of Amsterdam.

Most of these institutions reflected an approach to the Bible that ranged from conservative through fundamentalist to dispensational. Since World War II, however, at least among the older and larger Bible colleges there has been a deliberate search for academic recognition intended to enhance

[35] Anderson, *Guide to Religious Studies*, pp. 282, 309.

[36] See J. W. Grant, *The Church in the Canadian Era* (Toronto: Ryerson, 1972) pp. 60–65.

[37] Warren Charlton, "Dr. John McNicol and Toronto Bible College," *The Canadian Society of Presbyterian History Papers, 1977*, pp. 38–57.

[38] Private information of Ronald Sawatsky; see also Ben Harder, "The Bible Institute/College Movement," *Journal of the Canadian Church Historical Society* 22 (April 1980) 40–43.

institutional reputations, and this has led to the employment of younger university-trained scholars.

The Canadian Contribution to Biblical Archeology

Since World War II, the discipline of archeology has exploded in scope, methodology, and interests. Archeological work has expanded into geographical areas and chronological periods previously untouched by research, and new and highly technical specialized branches utilizing recent scientific discoveries and the latest findings in related disciplines have been introduced. Unquestionably, popular interest in the Near East has been promoted by the touring exhibitions of Tutankhamen tomb materials and by the romance and excitement surrounding the Dead Sea scrolls, to mention only two of the most obvious influences For biblical studies in Canada these developments in archeology have meant the employment of scholars in field operations on an unprecedented scale. Biblical archeology is concerned with the illustration of "the three-dimensional past" of events and periods of the Old and New Testament, in the eastern Mediterranean region (and as far as the Persian Gulf), and within a time span stretching from approximately 1800 B.C. to the fifth century of the Christian era. Related in varying degrees to biblical archeology are prebiblical and postbiblical archeology in the Bible lands as well as the archeology of Mesopotamia and ancient Egypt with their literary and cultural links to the Bible.

With the secularization of biblical studies through the creation of university departments of Near Eastern studies and religious studies, it was no longer necessary for scholars to have or obtain ordination from some denomination in order to be employed in their field of interest. Ordination continues to be a prerequisite for employment in some Canadian theological colleges, and the number of "seminary" and "non-seminary" jobs in Canada remains very small in the area of biblical archeology, but nonordained faculty among biblical archeologists, and biblical scholars generally, is more often the rule than the exception in postwar generations. Thanks to the burgeoning interest in archeology, Canadian universities now offer courses in archeology, usually taught by lay experts rather than, as previously, by biblical scholars with an interest in archeology. Many of these professors of archeology have, however, also had training in biblical and cognate languages, thus adding a philological dimension to their archeological expertise. From the archeological side they bring to biblical archeology new techniques, especially stratigraphy, which an older generation of scholars frequently did not possess.

In the years immediately after World War II the term "biblical archeology" acquired a pejorative connotation, implying to some that the sole interest of biblical archeologists was to prove the Bible true, especially in a literal sense. In reaction, some scholars preferred to call themselves "Palestinian archeologists." In recent years, however, thanks to new public interest in biblical studies, the term "biblical archeology" has begun to return to favor because biblical studies are now acknowledged to be more academic and less confessional, less dogmatic, and less apologetic than before. Indeed "biblical archeology" is now a term with advantage, since it is recognized that that branch of the discipline requires a breadth of background and interest not confined literally to Palestine. This renewed emphasis on the comprehensiveness of knowledge presumes a prior wide linguistic training, which has traditionally been a mark of biblical studies in Canada.

In the prewar period the most notable Canadian figure in biblical archeology had been William Ewart Staples of Victoria College. He had participated in the American expeditions to Megiddo in 1922 and in 1928–29 and had published about the site. T. J. Meek had been at Nuzi in Iraq, but his contribution had been philological rather than archeological. His greatest importance to biblical studies was his translation of early Mesopotamian law codes in J. B. Pritchard's *Ancient Near Eastern Texts* (1951).

In 1950 Fred Winnett, who was primarily a linguist, became director of the American School of Oriental Research in Jerusalem. He was attracted to Dibon, the site of the Moabite Stone, by hopes of finding further Moabite inscriptions and worked there for two seasons. With him in the second season was A. Douglas Tushingham, another Canadian who later served one year as director and who, like most American archeologists, had been trained in the methodological "school" of W. F. Albright. Tushingham continued to work at Dibon and subsequently published a volume on the Dibon excavations. In 1952 Tushingham joined in the work at Old Testament Jericho where excavations had been started by Kathleen Kenyon of the British School. As representative of the American Schools, he became Miss Kenyon's assistant there. Canadian collaboration with the British team at Jericho continued in 1955 and 1956, and although Tushingham did publish about this work his reports largely concerned the prebiblical period. Eight years after his work at Dibon, Winnett was again appointed director of the American Schools at a time of intense political unrest, and he showed himself to be a consummate diplomat as well as a very capable administrator and teacher. His last foray into biblical archeology came in 1962, when he assisted Dr. W. L. Reed with a sounding in el-'Al in Transjordan.

Kathleen Kenyon's contact with Canadian scholars had important results for biblical archeology in Canada. She introduced them to what may be called the "Wheeler-Kenyon" school of archeological methodology, which was subsequently reflected in the teaching of archeology in some Canadian universities. This shift in approach had political implications as well, since the British and French schools were closer to the Arab states while American official orientation and sympathy lay with Israel. For some Canadians the shift did in fact reflect a political as well as a methodological orientation.

The close association with Miss Kenyon also led to Tushingham's being selected as her literary executor. After the work at Jericho, Tushingham was appointed to teach Hebrew at Queen's Theological College, where he set up a museum. By the mid-fifties, however, he had moved to the Royal Ontario Museum, where he could pursue his archeological interests full-time, and between 1962 and 1967 he headed up for the ROM Canadian participation in what was to prove for Canadian biblical archeology probably the most important undertaking of the postwar years, the excavations at Jerusalem begun by Kathleen Kenyon.

Those excavations at Jerusalem had begun in 1961 as a joint British-French venture, but when the French withdrew the following year the ROM seized on the invitation to organize a large-scale Canadian involvement. Museum funds were supplemented by donations from University, Victoria, Trinity, St. Michael's, and Knox colleges in Toronto, from McGill, and from Waterloo Lutheran University (now Wilfrid Laurier University). Each donor was entitled to send a faculty member or senior student to represent that institution. In this way the Jerusalem project proved particularly valuable to Canadians because it provided on-site archeological experience to a number of promising younger scholars. Of two who came from McGill, William J. Power is presently teaching in Texas, but Robert Culley continues in biblical studies at McGill. At least four from the University of Toronto were involved over the seasons at Jerusalem (E. G. Clarke, D. B. Redford, R. F. G. Sweet and John Wevers). Redford has worked in both Egypt and the Holy Land, while another Toronto scholar, J. S. Holladay, has dug at Shechem, at Gezer, and in Samaria and now is deeply involved in the Goshen area of the Nile Delta, using "dirt archeology" methods to explore sites on the Exodus route. His work in the Wadi Tumilat is exclusively Canadian-financed and combines both the Albright and Wheeler-Kenyon methodologies. Among other members of the ROM staff who hold cross-appointments with Toronto's Department of Near Eastern Studies, at least three have been engaged in biblical-related archeology in recent years. A. J. Mills, N. B. Millet and R. J. Williams worked in Nubia, and T. C. Young, son of the sometime Victoria College professor who introduced Persian studies at Toronto, has been involved in the excavation of a Median site in Iran.

Canadian scholars were also involved, although somewhat indirectly, with the recovery of the Dead Sea scrolls. As representative of the American Schools, Doug Tushingham was part of an international committee established to acquire the scrolls and plan for their preservation, examination, translation, and eventual publication. Individual Canadians were involved from time to time in searches (sometimes physically hazardous, sometimes politically so) for other caches of documents reportedly hidden in the difficult terrain of the Dead Sea region.

After the announcement of the discoveries of the Dead Sea scrolls Canadian scholars and institutions were naturally interested in the possibility that some of the priceless finds might be acquired for Canada. In 1954 R. B. Y. Scott, on behalf of McGill University, negotiated a fifteen-thousand-dollar purchase from the Jordanian Department of Antiquities of scroll fragments to be known after the donor as "The John Henry Birks Collection." In 1955, Scott spent part of the spring in Jerusalem examining these materials, and in 1956 another purchase worth five thousand dollars was arranged. None of the materials ever reached Canada, however, because of political changes in the Middle East, and McGill did not recoup the purchase money until 1963. At that time the donor gave five thousand dollars from the total sum toward building a library collection of printed and photographic materials relating to the Dead Sea scrolls. McGill also acquired in these years archeological materials as a gift from R. B. Y. Scott's private collection of antiquities.

Although the archeological work of scholars at the ROM and the University of Toronto inevitably bulks large in the account of postwar research by Canadians, important work was also done by archeologists on the faculties of other Canadian institutions. From l'Université de Montréal Jean Gagne has worked on biblical sites in both Asia Minor and Cyprus, and Laval faculty members have also been associated with research and publication in Cyprus. Lawrence Toombs of Wilfrid Laurier University has been extremely active in archeological excavations at Shechem, Gezer, and Tell el-Hesi, and Hanna Kassis of the University of British Columbia has done significant work in Syria. Taken together, this biblical and biblical-related archeological research makes up an important and large part of the story of biblical studies in Canada since World War II.

Biblical Scholars and Publications

The immediate postwar years saw a veritable explosion of new journals devoted to biblical studies. Between 1946 and 1960 at least ten major new periodicals were established. Interestingly, no new titles were added in the 1960s, but the 1970s brought renewed publishing activity as five more biblical journals appeared. Canadians were prominent among contributors to most of these new publications, with a large number of their articles appearing in *Interpretation*, *Vetus Testamentum*, and *New Testament Studies*. Less frequently they also published in *Novum Testamentum*, *Revue de Qumran*, *Semeia*, *Journal for the Study of the Old Testament*, *The Bible Translator*, and *Catholic Biblical Quarterly*. Canadians continued their contributions to older established periodicals such as *Journal of Biblical Literature*, *Biblical Archeologist*, *Bulletin of the American Schools of Oriental Research*, *Zeitschrift für die alttestamentliche Wissenschaft* and *Zeitschrift für die neutestamentliche Wissenschaft*. Two Canadian Catholic scholars have been involved in recent years in editing *Biblical Theology Bulletin*, and another in editing *Catholic Biblical Quarterly*.

For Canadians probably the most important new periodical in the postwar years, because it was the most immediate, was the *Canadian Journal of Theology*, founded in 1955 "to recover and further the achievements" of the long-defunct *Canadian Journal of Religious Thought*. Despite this avowal of purpose the change in religious climate during the intervening generation was reflected in the title by its use of the word "theology," a deliberate effort to disassociate the new publication from the theological liberalism so evident in the title and contents of the *Canadian Journal of Religious Thought*. Biblical scholars were much in evidence in the management of the new journal. The secretary of the corporation was T. A. M. Barnett, and the board of directors included S. M. Gilmour, R. K. Naylor, Elias Andrews, N. H. Parker, and James D. Smart. The editorial committee had George Johnston as secretary and Robert Lennox, W. M. Kelly, Barnett, and Smart, while T. W. Isherwood was a corresponding member of this committee. The composition of the board of directors and of the editorial committee changed with the years but continued to be drawn overwhelmingly from Toronto and Montreal. The journal in its early years was also primarily a sounding board for English-speaking Protestants—the first Roman Catholic contribution was an article by Louis O'Neill in 1955. The first biblical article by a Roman Catholic scholar came from R. A. F. MacKenzie two years later, but the first article in French appeared only in 1965.

A sampling of curricula vitae of some members of the CSBS shows that since 1945 the periodical carrying the largest number of their articles has been the *Canadian Journal of Theology*—twice as many articles in fact as its nearest rival, the *Evangelical Quarterly*. In third place was the *Journal of Biblical Literature*, closely followed by *Vetus Testamentum* and *Biblica*. Next among some fifty titles came *Science et Esprit*, *Journal of the Evangelical Theological Society*, and then *Communauté Chrétienne*, *London Quarterly*, *New Testament Studies*, and *Revue Biblique*. Most of the articles appeared in English-language journals, but francophone Canadian scholars have usually published in both English and French journals. A very few papers by Canadians appeared in German-, Dutch-, or Spanish-language periodicals.

The pages of the early volumes of the *Canadian Journal of Theology* were dominated by the work of biblical scholars and theologians; only slowly did church historians and others begin to publish in the quarterly. In its first eight years the *Journal* carried at least one article on biblical studies in virtually every issue—on one occasion three of the five major articles were in this field. The most prolific writers in that period were Stanley Frost and Frank Beare, followed closely by George Johnston. Together they contributed half of the biblical articles printed. (George Johnston also contributed articles in other fields and was particularly active on the *Journal*'s executive through most of its life.) The first thirty-two issues contained no fewer than thirty-nine papers on biblical studies. All but one were by Canadians, but in the remaining thirty-two issues there were only twenty biblical articles. Two of these twenty were by Americans and virtually all of the remainder came from newer and younger scholars.

From about 1965 onward the complexion of the *Journal* reflected the growing ecumenical climate. Roman Catholic and French items appeared more often (but still infrequently), and more articles came from scholars not directly engaged in teaching. The excellent book review section had from the outset been a vital part of the *Journal*'s program and one which incorporated more quickly than the scholarly papers the current changes and developments in religious thought. Thus, in the area of Qumran studies, the flood of literature that followed the discovery of the Dead Sea Scrolls was reviewed critically and immediately, but the only contributed articles about the scrolls came from Robert Osborne in 1966. The *Journal* was particularly the vehicle for Canadian biblical scholars, more so in one way than for Canadian theologians since few biblical papers came from outside Canada, whereas authorship in theology for the *Journal* was more international from the outset.

Despite these developments there was a feeling that the *Canadian Journal of Theology* was not responding adequately to the broadening interests of Canadian scholars, especially in the new field of religious studies. The *Journal*'s circulation had not increased although several attempts had been made to attract readers among the parish clergy by increasing the number of articles concerned with pastoral problems. It was the formation of the new Canadian Society for the Study of Religion in the late sixties that brought the matter of the *Journal*'s future to a head. This new society proposed publishing another religious periodical, and many of the executive of the *Canadian Journal of Theology* were convinced that the limited academic audience could not or would not support two journals. Many of the younger scholars involved in the *Canadian Journal of Theology* were enthusiastic about the new publication venture, which would be multi-disciplinary and bilingual from the start—attributes that the *Journal* had never achieved despite conscientious efforts. Declining revenues, increased costs, waning support from the private sector and none from the public doomed the *Journal* psychologically if not financially. The coup de grâce for the *Canadian Journal of Theology* came with the Canada Council's decision to provide the new periodical with the financial support that it had denied to the *Journal* on the debatable grounds that in Canada public money could not, or should not, be given to "theology."

In a farewell editorial for the *Journal* Eugene Fairweather contrasted the Canadian intellectual climates of 1955 and 1970.

> Canada in the early 1950s offered little encouragement to the small group of men who there and then conceived and carried out a plan for a new theological publication. It

took more than a little nerve and stubbornness to go ahead with such an ambitious project in the face of unfavourable circumstances in the church and on the campus. . . . The academic theological community did not have too much encouragement to offer by way of compensation for the theological superficiality of our religious institutions. For one thing, most Canadian theologians were still working on the periphery of the world of higher education. With rare exceptions (mainly in the province of Quebec), biblical, theological, and other religious studies were excluded from the curricula of our major universities. Furthermore, the relatively small church-related colleges and seminaries where such studies were maintained were themselves separated by linguistic and denominational barriers. In a few Canadian centres of theological scholarship Protestants and Anglicans were co-operating in varying degrees, but they remained divided from their Roman Catholic neighbours, whether English- or French-speaking. Thus the *Canadian Journal of Theology* had of necessity to be launched in the impoverished form of a Protestant-Anglican, English-language journal, representing and serving a limited and fragmented scholarly community. . . . In 1970 a Canadian university which fails to provide for religious studies, Christian and non-Christian, invites the criticism that its curriculum is anachronistic and inadequate. In 1970 the Canadian theological faculty or seminary which tries to work in isolation from the wider community of theological and religious scholarship is on the way to becoming the underprivileged exception to a recognized rule. . . . The forthcoming journal of religious studies clearly meets a present and urgent need.[39]

The successor to the *Canadian Journal of Theology*, *SR Studies in Religion/Sciences Religieuses*, began publication in 1971, and its difference in scope and approach was declared and evident. 'SR will continue to serve scholars in the various disciplines who formerly looked to CJT as an organ for the publication of their work," announced editor William Nicholls. "But the special interest of these scholars will now take their place in a wider context of academic study of religion and religions by a variety of methodologies."[40] "The aim of the new journal will be to reflect this new academic and public respect for and interest in all the religions of the world, as well as a continuing concern for the religions which are indigenous to our own culture, Christianity and Judaism. *SR* will also give expression to the multi-disciplinary character of contemporary studies in religion. . . ."[41]

Although the CSBS was represented on the board of directors of the new Corporation for the Publication of Academic Studies in Religion in Canada (later simply Canadian Corporation for Studies in Religion), which produced *SR*, few biblical scholars were involved in the operations of the corporation at its inception. One acted as book review editor and two more were included on the twenty-four-person editorial advisory board of *SR*. A decade later biblical scholars were only slightly more in evidence; Peter Craigie was president of the corporation, but *SR* still had only one representative of biblical studies on its editor advisory board. *SR* did not carry biblical articles with the frequency that had marked the *Canadian Journal of Theology*, but this undoubtedly

[39] "Canadian Journal of Theology: 1955–70," *CJT* 16 (1970) 127–28.
[40] "A New Journal and its Predecessor," 1 (1971) 1.
[41] Broadsheet, undated, in possession of author.

resulted from the accessibility of so many new and specialized biblical journals and from the fact that space in *SR* had to be shared by biblical scholars, theologians, and historians with the numerous and active scholars in the broad field of religious studies.

Next to the wealth of articles published by Canadian biblical scholars in the various learned journals since the end of World War II, probably their most voluminous contribution has been in the area of multiple-author volumes and series. Frederik Wisse, before moving from McGill to McMaster, authored and coauthored no fewer than ten articles in J. M. Robinson's edited collection, *The Nag Hammadi Library in English* (1977). Canadians had been extensively involved in the production of the *Interpreter's Bible* when that twelve-volume work appeared in 1952. R. B. Y. Scott was one of the editors, and at least fourteen Canadians are numbered among the approximately 130 contributors. A decade later Canadians were less visible as contributors to the *Interpreter's Dictionary of the Bible*. Nevertheless, reviewing the *Dictionary* in the *Canadian Journal of Theology* J. T. Forestell hailed its appearance as "a landmark in the history of biblical scholarship on the North American continent."[42] It was, Forestell added, "a tribute to the ecumenical spirit of the *Canadian Journal of Theology*" that he, a Roman Catholic, was asked to write this review.

Seventeen of the approximately 250 authors in the *Dictionary* were Canadian, and of these five—Frank W. Beare, R. B. Y. Scott, G. B. Caird, J. D. Smart and S. M. Gilmour—had also been contributors to the *Interpreter's Bible*. Most of the others had died in that interval, and the rise of a new generation of Canadian scholars is underlined by an analysis of those writing for the 1976 *Supplement* volume of the *Dictionary*. Of nine Canadians listed in the *Supplement*, only one, R. J. Williams, had been a contributor to the original four volumes of the *Dictionary*, and for the first time a francophone Canadian biblical scholar, Jean Ouellette, is included among the authors of a major multivolume biblical series. *Peake's Commentary on the Bible* appeared the same year as the *Dictionary*, 1962, and had George Johnston and William Manson (a Knox College professor in the 1920s) on its advisory board. The Anchor Bible (1965) had only one Canadian contributor, prolific R. B. Y. Scott, who provided commentaries on Proverbs and Ecclesiastes. Among francophone scholars E. Beaucamp and I. Saint-Arnaud contributed to Volume 9 (1973) of Louis Pirot's *Supplément* to the *Dictionnaire de la Bible*.

Canadian biblical scholars have not in the immediate postwar years been as productive perhaps in terms of monographs published as their colleagues in other countries, but still significant individual works in both Old and New Testament studies have appeared from their pens. (The monograph series of

---

[42] J. T. Forestell, "An Event in North American Biblical Scholarship: A Review Article," *CJT* 9 (1963) 196, 200.

the Studiorum Novi Testamenti Societas, for instance, contains a quite disproportionate number of titles by Canadians. It would be unfair to mention specific Canadian authors of such volumes because constraints of space would require such a list to be selective and hence subjective.) One reason for this relative paucity of monographs may be traced to the smaller number of publishers in Canada and to their reluctance, in view of limited financial resources, to produce books on biblical studies and similar academic subjects, which admittedly have a highly restricted readership. This situation grew worse with the 1970s as economic difficulties drastically curtailed all Canadian publishing. Several smaller companies were forced to merge with larger ones whose interests are even more directed toward volume sales and away from the laudable but monetarily unrewarding area of academic publishing. To some extent, however, this regrettable situation has been offset by the development of a number of scholarly presses by Canadian universities and by the financial support of scholarly publication from such publicly-funded organizations as Canada Council, the Humanities Research Council (and the more recent government-sponsored Social Science and Humanities Research Council of Canada), and by the Canadian Corporation for Studies in Religion, which produces SR and sponsors a series of monographs in the total area of religious studies. Among the projects assisted in 1981, for instance, by the SSHRC were the production by the Université Laval of a French-language critical edition of the Coptic library of Nag Hammadi and the compilation and publication by the University of Toronto of a standard edition of the Royal Inscriptions of Mesopotamia.

In the nearly four decades since the end of World War II biblical studies in Canada have undergone revolutionary changes. The emergence of Roman Catholic scholars of international stature, both anglophone and francophone, has challenged the near monopoly possessed for almost a century by Protestants, Anglicans, and Jews. Equally revolutionary has been the growth of religious studies as a cognate discipline inextricably related to biblical studies. New methods in archeology, specialized interests—for example Ugaritic, Samaritan, and Septuagint studies—and the application of new technologies such as computer science have all expanded the scope and variety of biblical studies. The appearance of many new—and specialized—journals in the field has opened more avenues for publication to older and younger scholars alike. More recently New Testament studies have taken on a more positive and aggressive character as a new generation has seized on current scholarly methods and begun to examine the New Testament with the rigor and sense of excitement that characterized Old Testament studies in the past. These many changes and tensions have been reflected in the CSBS in terms of membership, programming, publications, and relations to other learned groups such as the SBL.

These various developments have seemingly fractured and diffused a scholarly discipline that previously possessed and cherished a high degree of cohesion and integration. Nevertheless, what might appear superficially to be confusion engendered by two generations of revolutionary changes in the field of biblical studies reveals on examination vitality, enthusiasm, and excitement that promise to ensure that biblical studies in Canada will maintain and enhance, in the words of T. J. Meek, "no mean place" in the international setting.[13]

[13] T. J. Meek, "Near Eastern Studies," *Encyclopedia Canadiana*, 1958, 7. 260.

RETROSPECT

In the century that has passed since J. F. McCurdy introduced the teaching of the higher—or as Canadians preferred to call it, historical—criticism at the University of Toronto, biblical studies in Canada have developed some distinctive characteristics or tendencies. To begin, the expansion of biblical languages as a service course for future clergy into biblical studies—a viable, specialized, and respected discipline offered in the university at the undergraduate level as an integral and desirable part of a liberal education—was a development probably unique in North American institutions of higher education. The fact that this occurred in University College—a secular, to its detractors even "godless," institution—might appear to be a pedagogical contradiction, but the peculiar Canadian traditions of church-state relations in education actually made this development possible. Canadians had already accepted the Victorian liberal premise that education could be based on "the general system of truth and morals taught in the Holy Scripture" without being sectarian or denominational.

These curricular and philosophical developments at Toronto were confirmed by university federation, since the basic principle of federation was that "secular" and sacred were sides of a single coin. In the Canadian understanding, a "wall of separation" is neither reasonable nor desirable. University federation also reinforced the teaching of biblical studies at Toronto by expanding the resources, human and material, available at that center. The most obvious result of this concentration at Toronto was the unquestioned, and for decades unchallenged, dominance or near monopoly that the University of Toronto and its federated members held in the field of biblical studies for several generations.

In terms of response to external trends in biblical studies, the influence of German scholarship, particularly of Franz Delitzsch and the University of Leipzig, seems to have been paramount in setting the tone and methodology of biblical studies in Canada. The methodology was rigorous and scientific. The tone was essentially moderate, seeking a via media and verifiable results as opposed to radical and speculative interpretations that would shock and challenge both scholarly and popular orthodoxy. Such crises as did occur in Canada over the introduction of higher criticism can be explained in large measure as a confrontation between a few somewhat indiscreet scholars and the moderate conservatism or liberal orthodoxy of both Canadian churches and Canadian society.

Considering Canada's close relationship and indebtedness to Great Britain and also the widespread influence of Scottish education and the "common sense" philosophy in Canada, it is surprising that Scottish, and also English, influences on biblical studies are so seldom in evidence. This may in part be simply a reflection of a lacuna in historical research, or it may be the case that German biblical scholarship did predominate in Canadian circles, just as the University of Toronto for so long overshadowed other Canadian institutions in this field. An ancillary and unanswered question is why Scottish influences were not more evident in biblical studies in Canada where Presbyterians and especially graduates of Knox College took such a leading role. As German influences declined in importance around the turn of this century the external focus of Canadian interest in biblical studies seemed to shift to that rising group of scholars in Chicago. This focus did not, however, last much more than a decade as other American institutions gained similar prominence and as the University of Toronto itself became a strong presence among graduate schools in North America.

Another interesting aspect of biblical studies in Canada—apparent until the present generation—has been the relatively slower development of New Testament studies. While this pattern has in a general way been discoverable in most countries and is explained by the more central and critical role of the New Testament in Christian faith, the Canadian situation may have been exacerbated by other considerations. No institution developed as a center of New Testament studies in the way that Toronto led in the Old Testament field, and that very concentration on Old Testament studies in turn narrowed opportunities for, and perhaps interest in, New Testament work. In addition New Testament work in Canadian institutions was more frequently taught by immigrant professors rather than native-born Canadians, and those immigrant professors sometimes stayed only briefly in the country.

In this respect the experience of Knox College is suggestive of the difficulties that might be encountered. In the space of twenty years Knox hired three Scots to teach New Testament. H. A. A. Kennedy, the first to hold the chair, returned to Scotland in 1909 after only four years; Robert Law died in harness a decade later; and William Manson, like Kennedy, stayed only four years before returning to his native land where he built an enviable reputation. Some of the imbalance between Old and New Testament studies has been rectified during the past generation, not only by the scholarly achievements of a new generation but also ironically by the development of religious studies, which has projected a certain element of relativism into biblical studies. On the one hand that relativism has attracted wider interest in biblical studies, while on the other biblical studies have been forced to compete for attention with other disciplines and with religious traditions other than the Judeo-Christian one.

In Canada no "schools" of biblical interpretation, whether centered on one person or on one institution, developed. Overall, individual Canadian scholars made their greatest contribution to biblical studies through their teaching. Canadian biblical scholars have produced many articles in their field—some have been literally prodigious in this area—but less frequently have they authored monographs. In international scholarly journals and organizations they have contributed as much if not more than could fairly and proportionately be expected from such a restricted group. Since World War II specific area interest groups, such as the groups dealing with Ugaritic, the Septuagint, anti-Judaism in early Christianity, and the book of Job, have emerged. The most distinctive and lasting traditions of biblical studies in Canada, however, are still the strong emphasis on language training as the basis of all further studies and that essentially conservative position assumed by most Canadian scholars in matters of interpretation, a position that J. F. McCurdy described as "a sense of proportion."

A NOTE ON SOURCES

Very little secondary material has been published on biblical studies in Canada. Only the brief article, "Near Eastern Studies," by T. J. Meek in volume 7 of the *Encyclopedia Canadiana* (1958) attempts an overview. The late John Macpherson's presidential address to the CSBS in 1962, "A History of the Canadian Society of Biblical Studies," was reprinted in 1967 by the society in its volume of papers, *Canadian Biblical Studies*, to mark the centenary of Canadian confederation. More detailed is the history of the Department of Near Eastern Studies of the University of Toronto prepared by F. V. Winnett and W. S. McCullough as part of that university's sesquicentennial celebrations of 1977 and circulated in mimeographed form. The development of religious studies in Canadian universities is largely covered by C. P. Anderson's ongoing series of reports on the discipline, which began with the publication of 1967.

Because of the central role in biblical studies played by the University of Toronto and its federated and affiliated universities and colleges the archival resources in that city have the most extensive collections of material relating to biblical studies in Canada. Nevertheless, the private papers of biblical scholars in those institutions have not found their way into the relevant archives except in the odd instance where the professors held administrative as well as teaching posts. The University of Toronto Archives, in addition to official records of the board of governors, hold the voluminous papers of President Falconer. More useful, however, for the long view of developments in biblical studies at the University of Toronto is the "Grier" collection or Graduate Record Files, which contain invaluable biographical data. The archives of the other Toronto institutions provide additional, if uneven, sources of information on their faculty members, and the archives of the Montreal-Ottawa Conference of the United Church of Canada, housed in McGill University, are particularly rich in materials from the several institutions that preceded McGill's present Faculty of Religious Studies.

Canadian historiography already possesses a good range of standard college and university histories and more are currently in the writing stage. Such histories provide general background information but seldom deal at length or in depth with the discipline of biblical studies. Two other valuable and as yet largely unexploited resources are denominational literature in the form of newspapers and periodicals and the journals which nearly all institutions of higher learning published in the late Victorian and the Edwardian years.

On the central issue of the reception of higher criticism in Canada W. G. Jordan's older article, "The Higher Criticism in Canada. II. The Canadian Situation" (*Queen's Quarterly* 36 [1929] 31–47), is extremely useful for its contemporary view of the troubles that befell the higher critics and "modernists." More recently, A. B. McKillop's *A Disciplined Intelligence* (Montreal: McGill-Queen's University Press, 1979) examines the intellectual and philosophical trends of the Victorian era in Canada, and Tom Sinclair-Faulkner has examined the question in depth in "Theory divided from practice: the introduction of higher criticism into Canadian Protestant seminaries," *The Canadian Society of Church History Papers, 1979*, 33–75. Other sources, both primary and secondary, consulted in connection with research for this book will be found in the citations of the notes.

INDEX